ALSO BY JIMMY BRESLIN

NONFICTION

The Short Sweet Dream of Eduardo Gutierrez

I Want to Thank My Brain for Remembering Me: A Memoir

How the Good Guys Finally Won: Notes from an Impeachment Summer

Can't Anybody Here Play This Game?

Damon Runyon: A Life

The World According to Breslin

The World of Jimmy Breslin

*Sunny Jim: The Life of America's Most Beloved Horseman,
James Fitzsimmons*

FICTION

The Gang That Couldn't Shoot Straight

Table Money

World Without End, Amen

He Got Hungry and Forgot His Manners

Forsaking All Others

.44 (with Dick Schapp)

THE
CHURCH
THAT
FORGOT
CHRIST

Jimmy Breslin

FREE PRESS
New York   London   Toronto   Sydney

FREE PRESS
A Division of Simon & Schuster, Inc.
1230 Avenue of the Americas
New York, NY 10020

For information regarding special discounts for bulk purchases,
please contact Simon & Schuster Special Sales at
1-800-456-6798 or business@simonandschuster.com

Designed by Dana Sloan

Manufactured in the United States of America

1   3   5   7   9   10   8   6   4   2

Library of Congress Cataloging-in-Publication Data is available.

ISBN 978-0-743-26672-7

ACKNOWLEDGMENTS

I have so much gratitude for the priceless help of Cork Smith, David Black, Stephanie Saul, Rita Ciolli, Eden Laikin, Carol Eisenberg, and Steve Wick. They report wonderfully well for *Newsday.* I also owe Ed Ward and Andrew Chaikivsky, and now there are too many people for me to repay in any form, so I won't.

FOR KELLY AND CHRIS

Noli venire inter Dominum et me

Prologue

What I am going to do now is invoke the special powers act of the first new Catholic parish in my diocese of Brooklyn since 1972, one in which I am in charge with the rank of bishop. Bishop Breslin.

I say bishop and not cardinal because I like the sound of Bishop Breslin. Just say it once and you know who's in charge. The big guy, Bishop Breslin. Kneel with your back straight and I'll give you my blessing. I cannot abide people slumped onto the pews like they're riding the subway.

I qualify for the rank of bishop because I'm not a pedophile.

In this match between Bishop Breslin and his religion and the old, established church, let me tell you something: The Other Guys Are the Joke.

And as bishop, I called my friend Danny Collins up one day and told him that he was the auxiliary bishop. He was extraordinarily qualified. Certainly, he is no pedophile or pimp. Let's get that out of the way. He does know Latin and Greek.

"Do we have vestments? I have no money for wardrobes," he said.

"No, Christ never had them."

"Good. You're not going to have us swinging a can of incense around?"

"Never."

"Because we get some free swingers and they'll wind up having pot smoking in the urn."

The idea of my being a bishop was outrageous and irresponsible and I loved telling everybody about it.

And then the pope called the American cardinals to Rome over their failure to protect children from priests, and that is quite a failure when you think about it. He called the cardinals to Rome because on his best days I don't think he knew where America is.

Afterward, the cardinals and bishops held two more meetings in America—or was it three?—in which they called for more thin air in which to cast their solutions to all problems. They formed a large national commission to investigate every complaint, pluck out all offending priests, and end the dark night. After some months, the bishops announced that they had determined that over four thousand priests had been accused of molesting ten thousand, mainly young boys, from 1950 until 2002. The head of the bishops conference, Bishop Wilton D. Gregory, proclaimed the scandal "history."

He no more can prove these figures than I can of my considered estimate of twenty-five thousand priests and one hundred thousand victims in those fifty-two years.

I know one thing. Gregory's church history cannot stand the light of a heavy candle. I issue mine after doing what he and his bishops don't know how to do: walk the streets of the parishes and listen to Catholics who, slowly, reluctantly, but so surely, tell of atrocities by priests on the young.

I was talking to my auxiliary bishop about it. "They are going to lose the church this way."

"They could," he said.

"Let people listen to them and then listen to me. I know what the religion has to do," I said. "You have to have women priests. And women from the outside, not restricted to nuns. Too many nuns need to have the past shaken out of them. All they do is bow to priests. The second thing you do is have married priests. A parish is a great job for a man and wife. Great housing. Sermons on Sunday. Major sermons. I'll write them with such spirit that they'll ring through the ages to come of Catholicism in America. The constituent work all week is the work of the Lord. You serve the poor, not the country clubs. Turn your parish into a church following the life of Christ."

I finished with my favorite expletive: "Beautiful. You mean to tell me that I don't have a better idea than the people in Rome do?"

"That's why I'm not going to do it," Collins said.

"Why?"

"Because it's too feasible and I don't want to get caught in it."

Chapter One

There is one tenet in which the church people are so driven in belief that they often can think of no other. They believe it is a certainty that their anger and fervor sends it off into the sky searching for God, and finds him. Abortion. Teachings and discussions of all other parts of life must be put aside, thrown to the winds, if necessary, in order to have full Catholic concentration on abortions.

The present pope has four subjects on his mind: abortion, abortion, abortion, and Poland.

It now is the official duty of these old men in the pulpits to cry murder at every liturgical function, no matter what the subject.

And so I went with my friend Ed Ward to a baptism on a Sunday afternoon on Long Island, at the beginning of the Hamptons. The church is a small wood structure that sat on this day on frozen grass. Ward was close to the family, including a young woman who was going to be married in the same church and by the same priest, your usual white-haired Irish. I stood way out in left field.

The priest poured water on the baby's head and the baby did not cry. This was a powerful kid. The priest finished the baptismal prayers and then said loudly, "Today, we are not only baptizing this infant and bringing Christ to him, but he is going to bring Christ to the world. Faith without action is unsatisfactory." The priest now began to speak directly to the baby. "And you"—he pointed to the baby, whose head now rolled in his white baptismal garments and looked right up at the priest, and with a nod that seemed to say he approved—"you must go out and stand up against abortions in the name of Christ and your church."

And the baby began to gurgle and roll his head and see who was around.

"You must stand up to these politicians who talk crap about abortions, stand up against this John Kerry who talks crap. He was for abortions and then he was for choice or he isn't for choice, you don't know. He talks crap. We today baptize this child and send him out into the world."

The baby was being told to go out into the world like a crusader. The average height of a crusader was five foot four, so on this day the infant didn't have far to go before a sword could be thrust into his hand. He would be on his way to do battle with these filthy murderers, these people who support abortions.

At the finish, I heard Ward say to the priest, "Don't you think it was a little out of context to be criticizing a politician like Kerry and then yelling about abortion? This was a baptism of an infant."

"Oh, no, it was proper," the priest said. "We have been ordered that at every liturgical ceremony, we must make a statement against abortion."

"Even at a baptism?"

"Yes. That is our orders."

That is one religion, the holy Roman Catholic Church. How could you not step away from such a church?

My belief always gave me feelings of indescribable beauty. In grammar school at St. Benedict Joseph Labre in Richmond Hill, Queens, in classes made larger by putting an extra row of temporary desks, the nuns built a brick wall of Roman Catholic Church faith around me that resisted all doubt. I gave my most precious belongings, a blind belief, one that was almost to the point of love of somebody unseen. It was young and fresh and it was going to be part of me forever, each day of my life a bright reflection of all that I was raised to believe.

Now the brick wall is gone and my feet scruff through crumbled masonry of a church that failed. The indifference and lying has caused me to look through the wreckage for these most precious belongings. I want to retrieve my promises, my vows. I know that I have my own heart, my own intellect. I need no stone tablet coming down from a mountain to tell me that I should not kill or steal. How can I be told not to have false gods in front of me when that is all the church does, throw up a false god, a huge building, and have you stand before it and worship something as false as a paper flower.

I need no person wearing vestments to stand between God and me.

I reach this place because I can write about it, and I should. I use anger, legitimate anger, too, at the betrayal by the church. What do you want me to do, say, well, it wasn't everybody who got molested, just ten thousand who have come forward? Then the church lies about it, and that suddenly exposes their entire structure for what it is, a fraud inhabiting great buildings.

But the nun dies last. The memory of her hand on my ear or hair is the only reason I sometimes still ask myself if I'm so certain of my belief that I can walk past churches like they were useless museums.

There was a late afternoon at the beginnings of darkness, with the East River across the street cold and motionless, and with a winter storm poised somewhere in the moody sky. I walked out of Memorial Sloan-Kettering Cancer Center after visiting my oldest daughter. She has a chronic blood problem which for ten years now has eluded research and which reacts to no treatment so far other than blood transfusions every fourteen days. Right now, she was all right and would be out of the hospital in a day. Still, it gets so long, so ominous for her. The expenditure of courage is stunning.

As I walked up the block, East 68th Street, I happened to glance at the Catholic church across the street, almost in the center of the block. It was the church of St. Catherine of Siena. She is one of the few Catholic saints whom I know something about. At one time in her life she opposed a pope. Good for her. In the years of going up this street I never have gone into the church. This time, deep in my troubles, I felt the church starting to draw me across the street. My friend Murray Kempton's rope across a slippery deck.

The moment found me at the intersection of two faiths, the Roman Catholic Church and the Catholic religion. They are separate and not nearly equal. The church sees holiness in a great big building. Then it produces pedophiles and pimps and lies and says we should forgive the priests. The hierarchy? Who are you to mention them? They are holy. About victims, confused and cringing twenty years after their humiliations and attacks, the church of Rome says we should pray for them, but first remember our poor priests. And beware of these people making allegations. They must be liars in a police station. They're claiming priests have done something wrong.

That's the one faith, the church faith.

On this day, here on 68th Street, I am waiting for my nature to direct me. The nun wins. I cross to the church. Inside the church, there was silence and dimness and low candlelight, all familiar, all comforting to my private prayer. Simultaneously, the scandals I have been writing of so much seemed to cover the floor and leave the church as dead as the statues. I was in need of my spirit being stirred and I got nothing. Of course I prayed. For a daughter. And I tried losing myself in a too-short prayer of love. Oh, Lord, give us your jobless, your homeless, your sick and imprisoned.

But the words in church are uttered into a confused air. Do I keep on in a church that I mistrust or remain outside and follow a religion I love? And right away on this gray afternoon, involuntarily, with no way to avoid the thought—I am back to the morning at the start of my daughter's illness. We were in a small room in the Dana-Farber Cancer Institute in Boston with my second wife, Ronnie Eldridge, my oldest daughter, myself, and Dr. Robert Mayer, an oncologist who had treated my first wife, my daughter's mother, when she came down with breast cancer that eventually caused her death.

Mayer had a clipboard and was asking questions. The usual: family background and illnesses. He answered the obvious ones himself.

"Mother. We know that.

"Father. Right here. Illnesses?"

"None to speak of so far," I said.

"Any surgery?" he asked my daughter.

"No," she said.

"Diabetes. Kidney. Liver. Heart problems?"

"No?"

"Pregnancies?"

"One."

It almost went right by me. My wife had her hand on my daughter's shoulder and they both were looking at me.

"What did you want? I was seventeen. Did you want another baby home?"

The church of Rome today cries "abortion!" to distract us from crimes by all their pedophiles and pimps. When this seems to exhaust itself, it turns to gay marriage. Look out that it doesn't make these the last two issues of their existence.

I got up and left St. Catherine of Siena. I'm walking out just for now, I thought. Then I said to myself, this church has stolen the spirit you need. Why would you go back?

A firefighter at the World Trade Center attack said something far more important than anything Rome says. He was around the corner from the first World Trade Center building to go down, Two Tower. He lost several of his people and was left against a shaky wall, dazed at being alive. A thick coating of dust made him a gray mummy. He did not say hello or recognize me with any motion. He just said:

"I have a daughter in college in Baltimore. And I love her."

He said this with tears.

And through the black smoke overhead were these words by cell phone, of the people of the fires who turned to final importance.

Stuart Meltzer, age thirty-two, on the 105th floor: "Honey, something terrible is happening. I love you. Take care of the children."

Kenneth Van Auken of Cantor Fitzgerald, on the 102nd floor: "I love you. I'm in the World Trade Center. And the building was hit by something. I don't know if I'm going to get out. But I love you very much."

Moises Rivas, a chef at Windows on the World restaurant: "I'm okay. Don't worry. I love you no matter what. I love you."

Veronique Bowers: "I love you, Mommy, good-bye."

Lucy Fishman, AON insurance to her home in Canarsie, Brooklyn: "I love you, I love you, I love you."

There were many hundreds of such messages, and all used the word that dwells in the souls of all on earth. Love. In the beginning and at the end, it is the vocabulary of Christ.

I was thinking of this as I walked downtown. It is the faith I'll follow to the last of my world that ends.

At this hour, Manhattan was a wall of Christmas lights. The

church has stolen some of the spirit from this, too. Christmas always was the Catholic church at its warmest, with the hymns in rich Latin, the people at their friendliest. Now they celebrate Christ's birth in a manger by holding midnight masses in palaces and with the priests in vestments that, if they are not made of beaten gold, they should be, because that is the idea of them.

The only time that Christ became angry was at the money changers in the temple. To me, that means St. Patrick's Cathedral on Fifth Avenue and the archbishop wearing capes and gold in a church as big as a mountain, and living sumptuously in a priceless mansion on Madison Avenue, right behind the cathedral.

At any church I run I will preach to the sky against the first evil of life, greed.

The church says sins of the flesh throw you into hell. I don't know where that comes from, nor is there any value to knowing it. When you start dealing with greed, nothing else counts. I want. It's the sin from within that kills. Why does he have what I don't have and why can't I have it? A church that is supposed to teach you to worry about the poor sets the standard for having, for owning, for rejoicing in great big things.

When you see the cardinal of New York, standing in the bright light and the vast, sweeping, phenomenal cathedral of St. Patrick, holding a golden chalice high above him as the gold on his hand explodes in the lights on the altar, it is now that you see the power of greed to spread. It covers an altar devoted to a man who walked on foot in sandals.

The start of my church will have no gold, brocade, rings or any other vain, useless, insane articles.

A gold ring on a bishop's finger is the commercial of a pimp.

Unneeded possessions step out of a church building and are regarded as vital to life: gold and diamonds for engagements or wedding anniversaries. Custom now has us by the throat and we cannot get out of its grip to figure out what we're doing with all this trash. Any church I'm around will give diamonds a bad name. How can you walk around with all these trappings in the face of people who have barely enough to eat?

The preposterous size and riches of church buildings is academic. Nobody should build them anymore. The archdiocese of Boston started selling churches to pay the victims of these priests of theirs, and of the bishops and cardinal who assign them to the biggest boys' choirs.

In this church I propose, all of them take a realistic pledge of poverty, and not one that allows you to use the riches of parishioners.

There was this freezing night when my wife and I passed the corner supermarket entrance, and walked toward our building entrance a few yards up Broadway.

"Do you think he was Christ?" she asked me.

"Who?"

"In the doorway. He was just standing there in the cold."

I stopped.

"Give him some money," she said.

I had none in my pocket. She went into her purse and gave me a couple of bills, one a single, the other larger, I didn't know how much larger, but I got to the supermarket doorway and there was this guy with a beard and a suffering face. The face was crinkled in the cold. He had a dirty gray blanket around him that dragged on the ground. You could see his body shaking under the blanket. The hands clutching it in front were raw.

The moment I gave him the money I knew I had given him the wrong bill. I had the single, he had the other bill, a twenty.

"My wife is going to call the police, and they'll take you to a shelter," I said.

"I won't go. They rob you in those shelters."

"Then where are you going to sleep tonight?" I asked.

"I usually sleep on the A train," he said.

"Let me walk you there," I said. He just had to walk down the steps at the subway kiosk two short blocks away.

"I can't. Two people told me to wait here. They were going to do something for me. I'm waiting here ten minutes."

"Then let's wait inside," I said. I ushered him through the sliding entrance doors. The moment he got a foot into the supermarket, a Latino checkout girl snapped erect at her register. "You go somewhere else!" she snapped.

Now two more checkout women looked up with fierce faces.

"He brings bugs!"

The homeless man who looked like Christ backed out. Suddenly, a lovely young woman, a willow wrapped in fur and fleece, came out. She had two plastic bags, which she put down at his feet. With her was a handsome young man, wrapped in black, his face covered with a plaid scarf.

"Now this is chicken in here," the young woman said. "And this is . . ."

I couldn't hear what she said now because the man who looked like Christ coughed loudly.

Then the young couple left and the homeless man who looked close to Christ looked down at the bags and said, "What do I do with these? I don't want chicken."

He had his sacks of coins ready to push inside at the right moment, and put them in the machine that gave him dollars.

"I want to get my money," he said.

"You can do that later. Let me get you into the subway."

"The money is more important."

"You have money. You could freeze to death tonight."

Now he looked at me with disdain. "Cold is a mind game," he said. "You can't handle that."

I was going to say something to him, but that long bearded face stilled my tongue. I turned and walked away. But now these street faces were in my mind. When I saw a homeless guy on the street the next day, I was almost sure of who he was.

Then I saw an ambulance parked on West 23rd Street with the back open to take in somebody. A homeless man was watching. Something radiated from him that caused my body to tingle. There was no question that it was Christ.

In the late afternoon, the freezing wind nearly cut off Christ's bare ankles and feet. When he was killed in Jerusalem, the temperature was in the sixties and sandals were common.

One of the people he loves the most was carried out on a gurney from a shelter on West 23rd Street. The man on the gurney looked up with a face the color of gray paste. Orange straps kept him on the gurney. "Seizure," a medic said.

The worst of winter fell onto the city that night and hunted through the streets for the helpless, for the defenseless, for anybody too poor to have a roof. For every other act, a blackout, the fire and explosion in the sky, the great city goes on. People come and go, they talk, they go to work. The homeless can go through the most miserable of rainy nights on the streets or under the archways or riding subways. But cold arrives in silence to torture. This night was the start of what might be the worst run of cold weather the homeless have had in this city. It was Christ's moment to be among them. The air clawed his face.

At six-thirty at night, he came out of the first darkness and swirling snow and into St. Patrick's Cathedral. There were homeless people asleep with their foreheads against the pew in front. They had hoods from rough, old winter jackets pulled over their heads. It was difficult to see how many homeless were in the church because there are fourteen great pillars that obstruct the view of the rows along the side aisles, where most like to sleep.

Sleeping in the pews on the main aisle is too conspicuous and thus an uneasy resting place.

Christ slipped into a pew on the side aisle on the left-hand side. He looked like all the others who had almost nothing. In fact, he had less. At least the other homeless people had plastic garbage bags filled with whatever they owned. Christ sat with nothing.

When he gave up his life for this religion, it was a belief that honored the blind, the destitute, the lame. Now he sat in a church and looked ahead, far ahead, over the many rows, to an altar that sat under a steeple and was dedicated to gold.

He looked up at a ceiling hundreds of feet high.

At the last pew, two ushers in red jackets stood facing the main front doors. For a while, a city cop was with them. When he left, another came in. Their hand radios kept saying something.

Christ looked and reflected. A man's forehead slipped off the bench in front of him, and he woke with a start. The man put his head down again and soon was back to sleep. A woman with a blue wool hat on talked to herself. Far ahead, in the front of the church, a woman walked around, pulling a suitcase on squeaky wheels.

They were in a place away from the cold, the most famous church of the Catholics in America. It is supposed to represent the Lord's religion.

On this cold night, one of the ushers said that the church closes at 8:35 P.M. Exactly.

And at a little before eight-thirty, a man on the right side stood up, yawned, stretched, and then gathered his plastic bags and walked down the aisle. He knew.

From far up in front, the woman pulled her suitcase on loud wheels. She knew.

At eight thirty-five, a cop and an usher walked around the church telling homeless people that the church was closing and they had to go out into the cold.

"Nobody can stay?" an usher was asked.

"Church closes," he said.

In the last row on the left side, a man stirred, then sat bolt up-right. He put on a blue wool hat and lifted a backpack that he carefully put on. He had two heavy shirts to fight the cold. He started out. People were coming from the darkness on the side aisles. Soon, the church was empty.

Christ slipped out of a pew and followed the other homeless people out of the church. The ushers and cops didn't have the slightest idea of who he is, and nobody running the huge church he was leaving knows anything about him, either. They claim they do. They say they pray to him and try to act in his behalf. On this night, he was asked to leave and go out into the cold, just like any of the other homeless.

"Watch yourself out there, it's getting very slippery," a cop said to all of them who looked like Christ, and one of them was.

Time and again, over all the weeks and months spent on this book, I was certain that one of the people I'm writing about actually was Christ. But I was fearful that if I said this, people would regard me as a new fanatic. I was afraid to type it because when I looked up and read my words I would think like everybody else, that I truly had lost my mind.

I will tell you how I got here and how much trouble it has been to write this book. Once it was known I was writing about the Catholic church, it seemed that every time I started typing, the phone rang with somebody telling a story that forced you not only to listen, but to go out and see for yourself.

When I got home one night, Tom Duane, a New York state senator, called to tell me I was going to hear from a person in his Albany office named Mark Furnish. Outside of Boston, where the *Globe* newspaper had a group of the swiftest news reporters covering the stories, there was no way of reporting the news of sexual atrocities by bishops and priests other than these phone calls that turned out to be true. Usually, a major crime report starts with a story for local news and television coming out of the police and a district attorney's office and then going on the Associated Press wire to the world. But on priest pedophiles, you had only these complaints from subterranean chambers where the hideous is buried.

The first news comes on the phone from somebody maimed by the past. It made the writing of this book extraordinarily difficult, for as you try to write, the calls keep coming, each one shaking you and demanding you shelve what you're doing and take up this matter.

Mark Furnish called a day later.

"Tom Duane asked me to call. I'm Mark Furnish."

"Where are you?"

"Albany."

"I'll come up. Let's see, what's a good day next week?"

"Let me tell you what it's about," he said.

"You can in Albany," I said.

"I want to outline it now."

He started to tell a tortured, slowly remembered story:

He was twelve and an altar boy at St. John the Evangelist in Greece, New York, outside of Rochester. The priest in charge of altar boys was Robert O'Neill. According to Furnish, O'Neill only visited the families of his best altar boys and, in Furnish's case, visit and have dinner and become friendly with the parents. Then he could safely ask the boy to come along with him on a trip to his cabin near the Thousand Islands of the St. Lawrence River.

It happens that just before his call, I had been going over notes about a priest with a house in the Pocono mountains in Pennsylvania that always was one bed short for the young group with him. Always one bed short. And Mark Furnish is on the phone about a shack near the St. Lawrence River. The style in each place and all the others was as unchanging as the collar around their necks. Everywhere, there was a priest at family dinner and a summer retreat or whatever to take young boys as a reward for service in the church.

"My abuser was a master of deceit and manipulation," Furnish was saying. "The priest knew I would not question his authority, especially because I'm in Catholic schools since kindergarten. He was smart enough to hide his sexual impulses under the guise of weekend trips with other boys at his cottage. It actually was a small, run-down, two-room hunting shack in the middle of the woods. It was three hours away from my home. I went on several of these trips. He took us to a local bar and gave us whisky, gin, and beer. Bedtime became one of the most stressful parts of the evening. One of us would be chosen to sleep in Father O'Neill's bed with him. Sometimes he would pick the boy to sleep with him, but most times we would be asked to choose among ourselves. If we didn't name somebody quickly Father would get upset and tell us to hurry up. He flipped a coin to decide. Father's bed was small. He said the only way I could sleep comfortably was to strip down to my underwear. He would not drop the matter until I did that. Then he'd offer to give me a massage so I could sleep. The massage would consist of Father rubbing down my body and always ended up by touching my genitals and buttocks area. Sleeping during the night was difficult. I'd wake up because Father's hands were touching me."

While no criminal charges have ever been brought against O'Neill, and a lawsuit against the diocese relating to his conduct was dismissed on statute of limitations grounds, Furnish was clear about the priest taking him in the woods for confession and the conversation turning immediately to masturbating. According to Furnish, the priest asked him how he masturbated and what he thought was the best way and then the priest started doing it alongside him in the woods. There were many more disturbing incidents which Mark successfully had, until now, locked away in his subconscious. He attended the State University of New York at Albany and became a lawyer. He married Kimberly, now a lawyer, four years ago.

He remembered that he and his wife were taking a trip into the upstate woods and emptiness that should have been exciting. Suddenly he had a panic attack. He had a sense of doom and he became light-headed, sweaty, and dizzy. Another time, his wife wanted to go away and they drove north again, and he felt he was on a train and not in control of it. He wasn't driving the train and he couldn't get off the train. Woods and emptiness rushed by him as the train went on, headless and evil, and he was close to fainting with anxiety. Sitting in a car.

In April 2002, fifteen years after the heinous acts of abuse he described, Mark Furnish, young lawyer, sat on the living room couch with Kimberly and watched television. They had on MSNBC, which had nonstop news coverage of the pedophile cases. They were watching heads who were talking about painful experiences with priests while growing up. They mentioned massages and masturbation and trips with altar boys. Mark's head began to close down.

"What's the matter?" Mark Furnish's wife, Kimberly, said.

"Nothing," Mark said.

"You sure act like there is."

Suddenly, he blurted out, "That's me."

Electricity went through his wife.

"It is?" Mark remembers her saying.

"And my wife said, 'You have to tell this. You can't keep this inside you and this priest can't be allowed to go without everyone knowing what he did.' "

He called me. It was the start of hurling it out of his system as much as possible. It also was glistening proof that the only sane way to go through life is with a dead smart, stand-up partner. Think Kimberly before you take the step.

After some weeks of trying to write about the sexual molesting of the young by priests, and as bishops and cardinals tried to conceal any fact, including their own involvement, my belief in my religion is deeper than ever. But not in their church. I disbelieve so much of what I am told by the church, including in this meeting in Rome in April 2003. It was a meeting of cardinals called in the Vatican by the pope to announce that it was wrong for priests to molest altar boys. That was his decision. Beautiful! It was dead wrong to fall on a boy. I went all the way over there to sit and listen to these church bureaucrats say, "We know and you don't," and then all they did was lie. Bishop Wilton Gregory of Belleville, Illinois, the chairman of the American conference of bishops, spoke to news reporters in an auditorium in the North American College, a building that sits in splendor amidst outdoor gardens a block or so up from St. Peter's. Gregory is of color. He was obviously smart and articulate enough to qualify for any job in the church. But he made you think of American television shows, where the chief of detectives is of color and that black face is on camera for the first minute and a half of the show, thereby proving that race has no place here: Look at him. He's the Boss. Are you saying we're prejudiced? He then disappears for the rest of the show and the white actors go on to enthrall Mississippi.

Gregory does last longer out front than television blacks. Simultaneously, the Vatican is trying to load the church with Africans to make up for dwindling whites while keeping the new African faithful in Africa where they belong, rather than strolling brazenly around St. Peter's Square, or Madison Avenue.

Bishop Gregory said that the bishops were trying to find a way to "synchronize" canon law and the civil laws in America. Here he was, he had come all the way over to Rome to put the illusion of papal firmness and solemnity onto the same cheap rules that got them into so much trouble in the first place. The bishops and some Vatican bureaucrats believed that they were beyond the law, that their own religious statutes, called *canon law,* allowed them to handle all transgressions as church business. This could let the church glide unnoticed through all storms. Crime by clergy was their business alone. They believed that. They really did. They were going to take their instructions from the centuries. Stall, confer, draw the thickest drapes until the room is dark and then tell you that there is a marvelous sunset outside.

Even the splendor of Rome could not suffocate the anger at hearing this. I asked Gregory: "Do you mean that you are trying to find a way to get around the laws of the state and city of New York, for which I voted, and use canon law, which I didn't vote for, and I don't know what it is?"

Gregory said that was not what he had said at all. He had merely said they were trying to find a way to "synchronize. . . ."

I said, "It's not a problem. Just open the door and let the detective in."

Bishop Gregory shrugged. His face said, this is exactly what you get from this rumpled newcomer; he's not even a Vatican regular. One Vatican priest, billed as a canon law expert, wrote, in an article applauded in the Vatican, that bishops in America should ignore the law and conduct their own investigations of sex charges. In a papal announcement meant to show anger and strength, the pope announced that pedophiles commit the grave sins.

He had to have a special meeting in Rome to announce that? Did that mean that it wasn't a sin until now?

Did that mean that it was not immoral before they had to call this meeting, and that it wasn't a crime?

The bishops at the Vatican advocated a phrase, "one strike and you're out." I don't know how they used such words because no-

body in Rome knows anything about baseball since Joe DiMaggio. I
do know that all were using cheap, trivial language to describe the
act of harming children. I am in the North American College auditorium in the Vatican when a group of women asked about their
right to be priests, and the lackey said the matter had been closed for
centuries. They were never to be priests. That ruling was infallible.
Thus there could be no discussion. The lackey at the Vatican made
this announcement without a hint of lying on his face. Why not? It
was not really a lie. He was only stating fact. The Roman Catholic
Church is an all-male club that is many centuries old and believes
prayers to God must be heard over the sound of women scrubbing
the floor.

I slumped into the seat and daydreamed and was lulled by the
sound of scrubbing. I pulled my head up with a start. Then it
dropped again. Suddenly, I am out of this auditorium and down to
St. Peter's and I walk into one building and then started winding
along halls and through great rooms with kneelers for prayer and
ancient and exquisite chairs and finally I am in this one grand room
and the old man sitting in a wheelchair looks up inquiringly.

BRESLIN (to the pope): I have an important question to ask you.
What is infallibility? Do you think that you are infallible? How do
you know that you don't make mistakes?

POPE: Infallibility is present only when the pope speaks *ex cathe-
dra*. And this we have not done.

BRESLIN: Why does the church hate women?

POPE: This is a monstrous untruth. We have the feast of the As-
sumption of the Virgin Mary. In August. She was taken into heaven.
She did not die.

BRESLIN: That is a delightful thought but I have trouble with it.
God bless her. She suffered. But I prefer to observe the holiday as
pleasant conjecture. I would remind you that it was Pius XII who

demanded such a feast. He was the pope who couldn't get excited over concentration camps.

POPE: We will pray for your penchant for accusations.

BRESLIN: Why can't priests get married?

POPE: Jesus Christ was a man. His apostles and disciples were men. If Jesus wanted priests to be married or women to be priests, he would have made them so. He did not. We uphold the tradition of Our Lord.

BRESLIN: On abortions, how can you place yourself between a woman and her medical doctor? Or a woman and her God?

POPE: A child is human from the moment of conception. The fetus cannot be killed.

BRESLIN: What if the woman's doctor disagrees? What if the woman praying to her God disagrees?

POPE: We believe that the church belief is that abortion is a murder, and Catholics commit a mortal sin by taking any part in such an exercise.

BRESLIN: How can you say that contraception is a deadly sin? You advocate a natural system. Rhythm. What is the difference? The intent of a natural system is the same as contraception. Therefore, what is wrong with contraception? You are accomplishing the same thing.

POPE: May we point out that as you have obviously done no formal studies of theology, you could not possibly understand the answer to this and the fundamental theology that validates it.

BRESLIN: I would like to ask one last thing. I am looking around at the splendor of this room. And of all the other rooms. And of the powerful view of St. Peter's, one that Catholics cannot imagine until they stand here and touch the walls of the Basilica. My question is, how can you and the others in your church live in this splendor when people are starving all over the world?

POPE: (UI) These initials mean unintelligible. He answered in high Latin.

LACKEY (suddenly walking in): We grieve for the poor. They are next to God.

BRESLIN: The rich surroundings give the appearances of the church not caring. That only riches hold their attention.

POPE: What would you have us do?

BRESLIN: Sell everything and live like Christ did.

The Catholic religious are supposed to live celibate lives. The word itself is confused with *chastity,* which means a pure life, virginity. *Celibacy* is defined as the passing up of unlawful or immoral sexual activity. But it does not describe a chaste life. The church will say to you, "He remained celibate [unmarried], although he engaged in sexual intercourse."

Only they could think this is clear. If you are normal, it is great reading for an institution dayroom. If you prance on the ridges of words, *celibacy* does not rule out sex. If they said *chaste,* they would mean absolute purity. Use of the word *celibacy* leaves a person with a life of their own, while letting the definitions get out there and mix the whole thing up. Celibacy, chastity, what's the difference? I'm pure! However, celibacy for priests arrives with three words: Don't. No. Never. Giving oneself up to honor God is the announced reason, but if you're Catholic, it's real estate. For centuries, the bishops, priests, and deacons were married and had families and lived on sweeping lands. They left the property to their children. One of the first and most urgent proclamations from one of the earliest gatherings of this religion, a council of Elvira, Spain, in 303, commanded that nobody could have wives. If they could not have wives, then there would be no children and, as there were no heirs, all land would revert to Rome. The church would steal it, but at least land would not go to some rat children.

It took a little time. Seven centuries worth of dissenting behavior had thousands of children who, after weeping bitterly at the funeral of their father, a bishop, went strolling about estates they had just inherited. Pope Benedict VIII, in the year 1018, decreed forcefully that priests could not marry and that their children could not inherit even a blade of grass.

The results of their forced celibacy show it has been an act of madness for the church. It leaves priests without wives and with masturbation. Or with an eye on the boys' choir.

When the American bishops formed a committee to end all sin, they named Frank Keating, the Oklahoma governor, as chairman, displaying hypocrisy as if it were part of their vestments. Their view of executions is distorted by almost anything. In the early years, the popes executed people for doctrinal deviation. The notion of such punishment was celebrated through the ages of Rome. The marvelous sound of a sinner screaming in the basement caused a great thrill to run through the whole Vatican.

While the church today says it opposes executions, and the pope sometimes says so publicly, the church has no serious opposition to executions. The American bishops argue against abortions and find that only the slimmest number of people do not yawn. They were so certain that it would be a brilliant political move to bring out Keating, a strong conservative, as a commission chairman in charge of cheap talk to show the public that they really were going to purge their molesters. Bishops, who had supposedly opposed death by the state, appointed Keating. Keating had presided over fifty executions and wished there were a lot more.

Here is a religion founded on capital punishment and it didn't stop to look up at a crucifix in church to realize this.

Keating made a politician's noise in the job, and unfortunately for the bishops, he made a politician's sense. He asked for the names of priests with complaints against them and the bishops thought he was getting personal. At the same time, Keating had taken a big job with the insurance industry and he was getting paid; the bishops might have been trying to pay with prayers. Whatever, Keating did not appear to put many hours in. Then he said that the bishops were as silent as the bosses in the Cosa Nostra. Keating didn't seem to understand that the church was in Italy.

So he was gone. He left the bishops with their principles shredded at their feet.

Chapter Two

B ack in New York after Rome, I decided that there were two ways to please my God and therefore get me to heaven. They appear to be contrary and yet either one might soften the path.

I could stay in the church and write with compassion and forgiveness and a reliance on redemption. Or, I could follow Christ's attack on the money changers in the temple. These cardinals and bishops in their gold splendor are the money changers. Follow that anger. Tell people what they don't know and what could hurt them. This would mean walking right out of the church, giving up the deep habits and beliefs of a lifetime.

Then, I went to an Irish mass at the Veterans Home on the campus of the State University of New York at Stony Brook. At the start of this day, staring from the early morning train at a heavy rain, I had an unobstructed view of both sides of the tracks. I could look ahead and here were big billboards coming up and then whisking past so quickly that sometimes I couldn't read the print. When the train came out of the tunnel from Penn Station and broke into the Queens daylight to start the trip, the courthouse handling narcotics cases was at the top of the embankment. It seemed that every few yards we passed a Catholic church or the neighborhood of one, most of them holding a part of my life. On the left there was St. Patrick's in Long

Island City and, after that, St. Sebastian's under the el in Woodside, where I went to my friend Norma Keane's funeral, and St. Mary's of Winfield, as this part of Woodside was called, and I attended a baptism of somebody I can't remember, and went to the Sunday basketball games in the church hall. The train ran across Queens Boulevard and through new attached brick houses in Rego Park, with Resurrection Ascension just below the tracks. I had been there for the funeral of Felipe Alfau. He wrote a book called *Locos* in 1936 that was overlooked for a half century and, too much later, he was nominated for a National Book Award. He was alone in a bare room in an old age home around the corner from Resurrection Ascension. He went to sleep hoping for death and was bitterly disappointed when he awoke. When he finally got what he wanted, I went to his funeral at the church, to follow a casket draped with lost potential.

The train now went past the Forest Hills tennis stadium, with its ivy walls, and the English village station square in Forest Hills, red tile roofs and brick sidewalks and streets running under arches, another place where nothing ever was supposed to happen. Of course it did. The two parishes are Our Lady Queen of Martyrs, a light tan stone church with windows like gun ports, rising from Queens Boulevard to guard the better-off. I went to mass there and my daughter Kelly was in their school. The other church was the red brick Our Lady of Mercy, on a street of trees and houses, where I buried a wife.

A few weeks back, my daughter Kelly suddenly said, "I don't know why they didn't go to Queen of Martyrs rectory and get Father Maurer."

"Who?"

"And Father Collins, too. I didn't know him as well. I knew Maurer. We hated him."

"Why?"

"Every time we had a party they had an altar boys' trip. None of the boys could come to the party. We hated the priests."

"Why did they take the altar boys away?"

"So they could fool around with them. What else?"

"What do you mean?"

"Molest them? Have sex."

"When was this? You never told me anything about it."

"I sure did. I told you a long time ago."

"I don't remember that."

"Then you didn't want to listen. I told you when it happened. Then I told you the time we all went to dinner a couple of years ago and I said something to Tommy Davis about growing up at Queen of Martyrs. He looked at me like I said something crazy. He was messed up. He's been messed up all his life because of that Father Maurer. And the other priest, Collins. Tommy was an altar boy eleven years old. He can't talk about it twenty years later."

"Was there anybody else?"

"I told you. Remember Michael? His father died. His mother went to the rectory and asked if a priest could counsel Michael. Oh, boy, could this Father Maurer do that. Then Kevin Kavanagh. Kevin didn't take it from them. Ask him. I'll call them for you. People should know what happened."

I later learned that a lawsuit had been filed by twenty-seven Catholics from Brooklyn and Queens alleging sexual abuse by Collins and Maurer as well as another twenty-two priests. Although Collins and Maurer of course denied the allegations, Collins has been suspended as a chaplain at a high school in Bensonhurst.

The train now went into the first of the thousands of true Queens streets of two-story frame houses with tiny front plots and a common driveway to frame garages in a cement backyard for each two houses. Off to my right was Holy Child Jesus on 111th, where I made the last mass. Afterwards, it was down to Jamaica Avenue, where you waited until the bar opened at one in the afternoon. You drank those cold beers with abandon and without noticing that suddenly the afternoon was gone and you were left with fog and guilt. One friend got married in that church in a hurried, but formal, ceremony and that was one that everybody counted months and, yes, the baby was premature. The people counting should have been annihilated, but that was life at that time.

Then St. Benedict Joseph, my home grammar school, and Our Lady of Perpetual Help, dances in an auditorium and at Christmastime I delivered the mail on those streets and a woman on 115th Street, Mrs. Swanson, let me come in from the cold and try to re-sort the bundles of mail that I had all mixed up in the carrier bag. It was all Christmas cards. The regular mailman carried everything substantial. One year I got tired of trying to re-sort the whole pouch so I put the tangle of Christmas cards in her cellar and said I would be back the next day. That day never came. I said a prayer for the friendships that I broke up. I really did. I said a prayer. I delivered the cards the next year, and nobody complained to the post office. About fifteen blocks to the south there was St. Teresa's, where I went to mass a lot and that was before they had a school, and St. Clement's, where we played ball in an empty lot. Now the train was under the platform shedrow at Jamaica, which had a five-story railroad building on one side and meat packing plants on the other. On the left was Presentation on Parsons Boulevard, where old men ducked in and prayed for good luck before going outside to the bus to the old Jamaica racetrack, and out the right-hand windows was the redstone front facade of St. Monica's, which had the easiest confessions for me. Then Immaculate Conception, where I went for Margaret Cuomo's wedding, and off to the far right was St. Pascal Baylon, where the only whites in the parish, Helen and Charles Breslin, in their seventies, who thought it was a sin to flee from people of color, helped run the church and then three guys broke into their house and murdered them because they thought the Breslins had the collection money at home.

Even the names of many of the churches where we pray and from which we are buried can be suspect. There are thousands of saints, many of them qualifying by martyrdom. All these people shrieking as they are being burned at the stake. The stories can be true and breathtaking. They also can be misrepresentations or tales tinged with voodoo.

Here was Joseph of Cupertino, who climbed to the top of tall trees in the night hours and then swung around the tops in the morning for all to see and claimed that he had flown up there. He became known as the Flying Monk. Somehow, he filled the requisite for the miracle of a saint. He became St. Joseph of Cupertino, but he was, for all time, the Flying Monk.

Since World War I, there were from three to five thousand visions in Europe. Only one lasted: Our Lady of Fatima in Portugal. A young shepherd said that the Virgin Mary appeared to her and said to pray for the conversion of Russia from godless communism, for this would bring peace to the world. A crowd said to be seventy thousand believed that they saw the sun spin in the sky at the little girl's request. She became a nun and left a letter with three secrets of Fatima. The first two predicted World War II, which sure was coming. The third is in a safe in Rome. In 1985, Cardinal Ratzinger said he and the pope had read it. But you can't. Later, they said the letter was about the attack on the pope in 1981.

At Lourdes in France, on February 11, 1858, a fourteen-year-old country girl, Bernadette Soubirous, said she had eighteen visions of the Blessed Virgin. Then a dry grotto suddenly spouted water and a rock that would be called Massabielle. She was told to drink the cool fresh waters. Soon, a basilica was built. By the fiftieth anniversary of the grotto, over five million had been there. Over four thousand were said to have been cured by the waters.

Time does not stop a vision that only one person sees. A forceful claim can take hold today as it did hundreds of years ago. Here in my time in my news business I am standing on 213th Street in the Bayside neighborhood and a woman named Veronica Lueken, short and with a high voice, spoke into a microphone while this big crowd stood in the street and clung to each word she spoke.

". . . I see an opening in the sky . . . Now, yes, now there she is. Oh, Our Blessed Mother is coming now through the sky. She seems to be hurrying. She is most anxious to give her message to the world. I know that from the conversation I had with her this morning at home."

She was on the street for twenty years, trivializing the memory of a woman who saw her son tortured and crucified.

Simultaneously, so many of these churches, or the next church over, has a dark tale to tell.

The train then went through streets of Queens, wood frames, with churches with grammar schools attached, rising out of the neighborhoods and into the Long Island suburbs. I got off at Kings Park. Late for the Irish mass being said in the cafeteria of the Veterans Home at the college, I slipped into a folding chair at a table and paid attention until it was over and then started talking to a man next to me. Suddenly a hand slapped on the table. Father Charles Kohli was sitting in his wheelchair and calling to the crowd in the dayroom of the Veterans Home at the campus at Stony Brook. He pointed to me, his guest at mass. "He loved his church so much that he is fighting against it to change it!"

"By being a bishop," I said in amusement.

"Certainly! Be anything you want. Just fight against them and change it all."

Then he said, "I am the last heterosexual priest on Long Island."

Another hand came onto the table. "You can do what we do. This is our church."

She was a nurse, with light hair and brilliant blue eyes. Her name was Sheila Muldoon and she was forty-seven and the daughter of a business agent for Local 3 of the Electricians.

"Mass right here on a card table. I spent twelve years in Catholic schools," she said. "I'll never go in one of their buildings. Not after what happened to us."

"What?"

"Priest J in the grand jury report. Nicholas Unterstein." (In the Suffolk grand jury report, priests were identified by case initials, not their own, as the statute of limitations had run out. This took people in parishes almost forty minutes to match the initials with priests and their victims.) "He came in here on a motorcycle. A Harley. He puts girls on the back of it and went riding. He was a big, good-looking, hip priest. He had a powder-blue Ford Fairlane. I never knew anything. We had a folk-mass group and he was right there with his guitar. He said to call him Father Nick. He was the first priest we ever did that with. You always used the last name. What a lovely, fun guy. He raped two sisters for six years. Donna Nichols, she was the older one, and her sister."

"How old?"

"How old. Thirteen when it started."

"He took everybody out for beer at the Wagon Wheel, Stage Coach. Henry's. He went to the Nichols sisters like a shark to blood. He never went near me. I wasn't vulnerable. I had a mouth. I was on picket lines with my father when I was five."

While Father Nick has denied the charges, he was defrocked.

"They moved him around. He left the church and got married. I think he's in Oceanside. After him, we had this old pastor, Alfred

Soave. He had a history with boys. Boys started complaining that he asks bizarre questions. They moved him out. So we had our scandals both ways, girls and boys."

She looked out over a dayroom filled with old soldiers in wheelchairs and with canes. They had just held mass, seated at card tables.

"I'll never go back to one of their buildings," she said again. "My husband says we can put up a tent in a parking lot and say mass. And here, we use card tables. I'm a nurse here but I never work weekends. I was not attending mass in my regular parish. My husband comes here to see his father. They go to mass here. He came home one time and said I have to be with him the next time. My husband said that the priest really puts it out there. So I came here. Sitting at a card table. He says mass right over there against the wall. Father Kohli called out the bad priests and said that they should be thrown out of the church and arrested and put in jail. I came the next week and he was on it again. We never heard anything like this. All they said in our church, St. Hugh of Lincoln, was that we should think of all the good priests who do such good work and not let a couple of bad ones distract us. They were even building new churches. Can you believe that?"

There were two large churches in her area, and suddenly they were replacing them with two big new buildings. The cost was astronomical. It is as if there was no problem. Sheila Muldoon could no longer understand her church. When they build a new church atop the oldest and worst of all sins, she thought it was time to walk off.

Chapter Three

I am on my way to church on a Sunday, as I've been doing every week since age seven. If at any time I failed to go, I don't remember it. Everything is different now. What am I, a sucker? Going to a church. The only reason I am going to church is because at the moment, even with all I've seen and heard, I still live in indecision and don't know anything else to do on a Sunday morning.

I am walking toward the eight o'clock mass at Blessed Sacrament Roman Catholic church on West 71st Street, between Broadway and Columbus Avenues, on the West Side of Manhattan. It is around the corner from where I'm living now.

Broadway was empty on this morning in late spring. One bus rustled the stillness. It passed by slowly, rocking, small rattles coming from the doors. Off to the left were the buildings of Lincoln Center and past them, the square, gray tower of St. Paul's, the only church in sight, a Catholic church, which doesn't seem to fit the West Side, which is far more secular than what I grew up with. Out in Queens, the sound of my religion always was a soft, lovely murmur of the footsteps of the faithful walking to mass at a few minutes before each hour on Sunday mornings. In all my Sunday mornings everywhere I've been, no place since then has been so dominated by a religion. Here, this morning, I make the only sound.

You would recognize the West Side streets from any of the hundred movies and television shows that have been filmed on them. Seventy-first street, however, begins with a building that evokes the feeling of being in Europe, in Rome. You won't even miss the architecture of Rome if you split the American Catholic church from the Roman, which has to be the subject of any legitimate discussion of today's Catholicism.

On the northeast corner of Broadway and 71st Street is the Dorilton, a Beaux Arts apartment house that was built in 1902 by construction workers who qualified as sculptors. The Dorilton entrance has ornate iron gates and sculptures of two girls. Gates open to a small courtyard and front doors that are framed by cement scrolls. A person feels uneasy entering without being in formal attire. The building has two wings and you look nine stories up to see a spectacular arch that walks across the sky from one wing to the other.

Next to the Dorilton are four attached four-story brownstones, with a couple of steps leading down to the front door, actually the basement entrance, which in this suffocatingly expensive West Side living, becomes the first floor. Visitors tingle with thoughts of actually living here. They enter long narrow rooms whose walls speak Manhattan.

On the other side of the street is an apartment house that once was a hotel where Babe Ruth lived. You could imagine Ruth's bellow right now as he came out. That glorious sound would be lost today in the multiple collision of fire-engine horns, cab horns, trucks shifting gears, sirens, loud cars, dogs barking.

Blessed Sacrament church, next door, was built in 1917 and has the cement scrollwork of the age of labor by talented hand. It is as meaningful as a church can get. It has homeless asleep in the pews, a soup kitchen serving out of the grammar school at the rear of the church, and a basement for stage plays. I have never walked in or out of this church without a feeling of warmth and thankfulness. Until now. The fault is not in this particular building or the friendly people in it. It is what it represents: the church of Rome.

It has six large front doors that are kept open most of the time, and the street noises, as if in reverence, fade in the doorways. Inside in the coolness, I kneel and say a prayer. If I'm in a church, I do what you're supposed to do in a church.

Hanging over the brightly lit altar from a ceiling that is nearly four stories high, is a crucifix that might be the largest in my city. It is twenty feet tall and weighs hundreds of pounds and it has been here, in Blessed Sacrament, for a half century.

On one thoughtful, lovely September day twenty-two years ago, Ronnie Eldridge and I were married on the altar under the crucifix.

Ronnie also wanted to be married by a woman rabbi, Helene Ferris, at Stephen Wise Free Synagogue, around the corner from where she lived. The head of Stephen Wise, Rabbi Balfour Brickner, being a locally famous liberal, would not let Irish Roman Catholic Breslin be part of such a ceremony in his temple. Some of Eldridge's friends said, "Wait until you see what happens when you go to his side."

My side, a priest on the staff of the cardinal, offered a famous chapel in St. Patrick's Cathedral or, if we wanted to plan the date a little better, the main altar. The priest said that the church considered our marriage a reaffirmation of faith by both people. There were going to be no children in the marriage, so they could be tolerant. We decided on Blessed Sacrament church, with an old friend of mine, a dear friend, Monsignor Jack Barry, performing the ceremony, with a rabbi who was an old friend of Ronnie's and her family, Rabbi Martin Zion, coming to the apartment for a second ceremony. He asked that we not put his name in any newspaper notice. I would have regarded this as a lifelong insult, but then his son was killed in the World Trade Center attack and I am grateful for not having made one of my usual remarks.

Monsignor Jack Barry arranged our children at the altar. My wife had died a year and a half earlier and Ronnie Eldridge's husband had died twelve years earlier. I had six Queens Catholics. Eldridge had three West Side Jewish.

Emily Eldridge, nineteen, looked up at the crucifix and said to herself, "Wow. That is a big Jesus Christ."

She spent the rest of the ceremony afraid that the crucifix would fall and kill everybody.

Now on this Sunday twenty-two years later, I had a little task at this mass, passing the collection basket. I have been doing this for two years, quietly and pleasantly, with no thought of it being anything other than a small gesture, too small to qualify as a service.

Everybody stood and recited the prayer entitled the Nicene Creed, and it was right here, for the first time, and as a result of all the news each day, that I found myself not only questioning, but disputing, the prayers as I recited them. You are not supposed to question what you are saying. Just say it. Who are you to hesitate over sacred words passed down through the ages? This time, I examine how and where these prayers come from.

> *For our sake he was crucified*
> *under Pontius Pilate . . .*
> *On the third day he rose again . . .*

In my entire time, from grammar school when I learned it until today as I start to recite it again, the words after "Pontius Pilate" said,

> *He descended into Hell. On the third day . . .*

We used to wonder in silence about the "descended into Hell." What was that about? He had just suffered crucifixion. Now what happens? Christ in flames? Suddenly, this morning I realized that the "descended into Hell" had been removed from the prayer without an announcement. I doubt many Catholics have noticed. What do you want from them? They pray without hearing their own words.

On the page following the Nicene Creed is the Apostles' Creed, the exact same prayer as the Nicene Creed except for this:

> . . . *he suffered under Pontius Pilate,*
> *was crucified, died and was buried.*
> *He descended to the dead.*
> *On the third day . . .*

I have no idea what "descended to the dead" is about and I am certain that neither does anybody else in the church.

I read something by a French playwright, Paul Claudel, out of the French Catholic Renaissance in the early 1900s, who wrote about Christ descending into hell, but what hell was it? First, Christ rips open purgatory and releases the millions of captive souls. Claudel mentioned once the penal flames, but concentrated on describing a pit of corruption, a larder of corpses, this morgue, this warehouse of corpses, this garden of skulls, this valley of the shadow of death. By descending there and then leaving, Christ gave the physical sense of the absence of God, and that is punishment forever. Claudel gives hope by writing, "The father does not abandon his child at the bottom of the well."

All this scholarly work by a great Catholic has been wasted. The church took "descended into Hell" out of the books. In all the printings in all the languages, the phrase is out.

However, in the spring of 2002 I was in church in Phoenix, St. Thomas's in the rich section of town, and the priest led the congregation in the Apostles' Creed and sure enough they had Christ in hell. Perhaps they didn't change it because their good Bishop Thomas J. O'Brien was too distracted from his duties by the sexual molesting being done by priests, whom he kept moving about to prevent insurrection by the people. Finally, he would plead guilty in public to obstruction in exchange for no jail time. He then took what we always thought was the Irish answer to heartache, the drink. It killed his senses. He was driving drunk when he killed a man and tried to flee. Of course he was caught. He resigned and the pope promptly accepted. He was convicted and the court let him walk.

I believe that much listed as religious scholarship is actually purported scholarship: St. Jerome, translating a description of Moses in 405, confused roots and the word halo became horns and Michelangelo, reading from this as if it were a recipe book, sculpted his magnificent statue of Moses with horns and not a halo.

If scholars make such mistakes, you can only imagine what some illiterate fishermen, translating through several languages over a hundred centuries, tell you to believe or get burned to a crisp. I was rescued by a book by John L. Allen, Jr., who writes out of the Vatican for the *National Catholic Reporter* in Kansas City, and I make him the most knowledgeable and literate of anybody dealing with religion.

He writes of a Swiss priest and philosopher, Hans Urs von Balthasar, who had a girlfriend, Adrienne von Speyr, a medical doctor, who convinced her boyfriend that she could see the "dark night" and "descended into Hell" was real because Jesus went down there to bring out Abraham and Moses, who were there because they never had seen Jesus. When Jesus removed them, he left hell empty forever. A lunatic teaching lessons in lunacy. When she died, he waited twenty years and then suddenly announced that Christ's descent was the final abandonment by the Father, that Christ actually suffered in hell with souls who had refused God. The "descended" remained in the books of prayers until a Vatican committee, large enough to staff the city of Rome, took years to make the changes about "descended into Hell" and then did so in secret.

I regarded anything they did in Rome with this as just more of their cheating. They found themselves without a defense for an old, crazy idea and now that you had believed it for life, they simply whisked it away as if it never was there. They were trying to slip something past a Catholic like me who had been taught all through grammar school to fear hell and who, in case I hadn't been frightened enough, had read James Joyce. He was some sick man, Joyce was, I'll tell you that. He wrote that you get in a chamber of hell and you can hear nothing but the shrieks of suffering. The place is the blackest of black and your body is afire with flames that burn but do not consume. You can't even burn to death. This lasts for eternity, which is thousands and thousands of millennia and after that it truly begins and never ends.

It was at this point in the mass that I looked at the missalette, the paperback guide for the masses of the season, and I read some of the prayers:

> Oh, God, you are my God whom I seek,
> for you my flesh pines and my soul thirsts
> For your kindness is a greater good than life . . .
>
> My lips shall glorify you . . .
>
> Lord God, heavenly King,
> almighty God and Father,
> we worship you, we give you thanks
> we praise you for your glory.

This brought something out of me that I have kept hidden for all of my life this far. Why, if God knows who he is, do these miserable

creatures on earth have to run around calling out his name in admi-
ration, extolling him with each sentence, singing his praises to the
exclusion of all other thoughts: "How Great Thou Art."

Is this all you can do to honor him? Christ was a carpenter. He
must have started work at about age ten, which is how it went in his
day, and then at thirty he went out on the trail. But that is twenty
years as a workingman. Christ with saw and hammer, working with
his father. Can't you gain any inspiration from that? Don't you have
anything to say about it? I think he was saying more to us by his example of work than we say to him with prayers telling him of his
glory and power.

I said to myself, you sit down someplace and write new prayers
that will attempt to touch people. Nobody can be moved by the rep-
etitious adoration. I think a prayer about a carpenter, or the meaning of a carpenter, would send little sparks into the mind, their
brief bright light and warmth causing different thoughts, swifter
thoughts, more meaningful thoughts. No more glazed prayer. It was
obvious that the start of a prayer had to do something with sawdust.

Now I turn and poke the collection basket in front of the people in
the first row. Rose Fiordalisi is first. She is a woman in her late sixties
and has short dark curly hair and she interrupts her prayers to smile
beautifully and put an envelope into the basket. On election days she
is a poll inspector in the public school on the other side of Broadway.
One election night she told me sorrowfully that her daughter had
just died at age thirty of a burst aneurysm. She told that to me because I just did beat an aneurysm. Everybody told me to get to a doctor in Phoenix, Robert Spetzler, who had performed by far the
largest number of these dangerous operations in the world. He
opened my head like a trapdoor and saved my life. Rose Fiordalisi's
daughter had been helpless with headaches, and was on the table for

an MRI of her brain. "She freaked out. The claustrophobia. She got off the table," Rose said. The daughter dropped dead in fifteen minutes or so. "They said they could've seen it in time with the MRI," Rose said.

If I didn't have to move on with the basket, I would've leaned in and whispered to Rose some utterly lousy but highly interesting and vicious gossip: about the Catholic chaplain in Phoenix who came into the room just before I went into the operating room. I remember the night before that operation. I was alone in the room and looking out the window at the streetlights on the wide empty street, Third Street in Phoenix, and I had no fear and no nerves, and I knew I could just get into bed and fall asleep. I was sure that this was because I was in the state of grace and that it came from a lot of years of writing about the poor. They were my daily prayer. Then when I got up in the morning I couldn't wait to say a prayer with the priest and go in and get my head cut open.

The priest and I and my wife and daughter held hands in a circle and said a prayer. Then with a sincere handshake and murmur of God's help, the priest left.

"Lord, isn't that something," one of the doctors in Phoenix said on the phone just the other day, mentioning the priest.

"What?"

"I'm afraid he isn't here. He had a little problem."

"What?"

"One of these pedophiles."

All these reminders and memories do is confuse. Pedophiles. The word is in my ear as I move to the next row. Why am I even here? Of course there were reasons I went through the rest of the collection. There was the young boy, ten or maybe less, in the fifth row with his family, and they always give him a dollar to put in the basket and he can barely wait each Sunday, standing in the pew, eyes gleaming, as I come up and hold the basket just out of his reach, and as he strains, I pull the basket farther away until, as he does this week, he falls onto the father next to him as he reaches out to get the dollar in.

After that, there were these people who put the money in mechanically, while concentrating on the mass. The priest was at the offertory and that is one of the three principal parts of the mass.

At the rear row, here was a man with a blind young woman who had a beautiful smile. He dropped a bill in and then guided the young woman's hand as she put change into the basket. I dumped the money into the head usher's basket and stood my wicker basket against the holy water font.

I wanted to leave right there, but I had a doubt about doing this in the middle of mass. If the nuns at St. Benedict's told me it was a mortal sin to miss mass, then that's what it was. That's the kind of knowledge that does not go away, ever. You had to be paying strict attention, daydreaming is a sin, for the three principal parts, the offertory, consecration, and communion. Italian men in my old neighborhood knew more than any of us. The men at St. Pius stayed outside and smoked cigarettes while the women were inside praying. The men had a good chance of going to hell, we always thought. Palm Sunday was different. Even the men went inside. They took strands of palm and broke them into small crosses, which they stuck in the hatband or pinned to their suit lapels. The women had palm crosses on their shoulders.

All these years later, a bit late for anybody I know, you find that missing mass is not actually a sin. There was never even a penalty for missing the Gospel. The sermons that follow show that Catholics lean to boredom. It is all on paper. You cannot write with much spark unless somewhere in your early years you have rebelled. These priests have done nothing but conform. This leaves you with dreary sentences that the priests match with dolorous tones. I have been a now-and-again sermon resister from my time in grammar school.

If I had one shot at delivering a sermon, I would have them rising from the pews and interrupting me with crescendos of applause and shouts of "Good boy, Bishop Breslin!" for I would not come out there in the usual style of priests, who put ideas in big letters on index cards and then drone on for a half hour. I would have a tightly scripted and rehearsed sermon that would be on something new and vital. I cannot tell you right here what one of my sermons would be about, because these thoughts right here are for a book, for thoughtful reading at a time of your choosing. At the same time, I know they would be about a house mostly. Evictions belong in the pulpit. My sermons would be of the moment, with names and addresses of the poor who are suffering, and with finger-pointing, shouting at the parishioners that it is their responsibility before their God to help these people. Don't worry about me. While my ambition may be difficult to put into effect, it throbs with noble energy.

With the collection over at Blessed Sacrament on this early Sunday morning, I stood against the wall, a step away from the doors.

I thought about my Aunt Harriet. Anything I have to do with religion is going to follow whatever she does. She had the strongest faith of anybody I've known then and since. I was raised in an unattached frame house on the corner of 134th Street and 101st Avenue. Next to it was a large old warehouse that had rats scurrying in and out of it. Eight Catholic churches were only a walk away. I lived in the house with my mother, sister, grandmother, two aunts, and two uncles. My father left on foot when I was seven.

My Aunt Harriet's neighborhood Catholicism grew stronger wherever she went. She graduated from Barnard College in Manhattan, and was working in the city for a year maybe when she married Peter Arnone, who was twenty-one and had just been drafted. This was in 1941.

He had a furlough in December 1941 and on December 7, Sunday, they were at the baseball game between the then New York Giants and the then Brooklyn Dodgers at the Polo Grounds when the loud speaker called out, "General Donovan, please report to the head usher." The announcement was made several times. When my aunt and Peter Arnone got home to Richmond Hill they were talking about how people around them at the game were saying, "That's Wild Bill Donovan." At that time, he was the best-known American military man. She and Peter Arnone had listened without surprise. They knew what it meant. What did Donovan have the uniform on for, in case there was no war? When they got home and were listening to the radio in the living room, they still never thought that they were about to lose so much of their young lives.

You can say today, "World War Two," or "WW2TheBigOne," as Archie Bunker did. Neither way describes five years lost.

Peter Arnone was sent to Camp McCoy, outside of La Crosse, Wisconsin. My Aunt Harriet threw up her office job and came home and packed a suitcase. She left on a wartime Sunday night. I was going to carry the suitcase to the train. I remember she knelt at her bed and prayed before going. She was twenty-one and she was going to use those prayers and belief in them to get through a war. Oh, this was no religious fanatic. She took a drink, don't worry about that, and the best picture I have of her shows her eating a hot dog in the grandstand at the old Jamaica racetrack.

I remember carrying the suitcase that night. We got on the Q-8 bus on the corner of Van Wyck Boulevard, which was then a narrow street. We got off at the Long Island Railroad Station at Sutphin Boulevard, and I lugged the suitcase up two flights of stairs to Platform One, the trains to Penn Station. We were in Penn Station

twenty minutes later. We came up one flight and walked to the end
of the long lobby to the IRT subway. There was another flight of
stairs up to the platform. We rode the train one stop to Times
Square. I remember that by now the suitcase was bringing my
shoulder down so that it barely cleared the floor. I was proud I was
doing it. She was going off to war and I was part of it. We got on the
shuttle that went for one noisy swaying run crosstown to Grand
Central station. Up another flight and through another struggle to
the station, which was crowded with uniforms in the half light and
black wrought-iron platform marquees with their train destinations
in red and the times in white.

I bumped the suitcase down the staircase. She got a seat in a car
that rapidly filled. Another ten minutes and she would have been
standing for the day and a half to Wisconsin. Perhaps more, since
trains were regularly sidetracked to make way for troop trains. I
brought the suitcase up against my chest and heaved and pushed it
onto the overhead rack. I had just done something important. She
had rosary beads in one hand and as the train left, she was smiling. I
didn't cry because I felt so good about what I had done.

She wrote me a short note from La Crosse, Wisconsin. To me, it
was as far away as the Arctic. She had a room and saw her husband
when he got a pass. She said that she had seen a cousin who worked
for the Fanny Farmer candy company. I wrote Peter Arnone and
asked him how he used the sight on the M1 rifle. He wrote me back
about clicks. Then his unit was shipped out. My aunt came back to
101st Avenue with that big suitcase and I dragged it upstairs and she
unpacked it and put it right under the bed. She was ready to move at
the first letter. I was thinking of this now. I was thinking that her life
could be the example for me. How she carried the Catholic religion
could virtually direct me. She was too smart and practical and filled
with love to let her church's voodoo distract her. And she was too
strong to let her mind swing about in thoughtlessness.

A philosopher, Lucretius, is often quoted: "Religion has brought forth impiety and crimes."

Aunt Harriet disagrees. "The church brings out impiety and crime. The religion is mine, and I don't commit crimes."

Now, with the mass still on, I dipped my hand into the holy water, blessed myself as I've done since early grammar school, a habit that is here forever. I quietly slipped out of the church and onto the Sunday quiet street. I was neither sure where I was going nor how long I would be.

Chapter Four

On a Sunday afternoon, I stopped in Forest Hills in Queens to see Arlene D'Arienzo and her husband, Nicholas. Arlene is a beautiful, willowy woman who does not obscure the fact that she has her own mind. Her house always has been one of the great pleasures. Nick D'Arienzo is a doctor and is as devout a Catholic as I've known, and as cheerful as anyone can be. Everybody from everybody's family walks into his kitchen to ask about anything from a shoulder pain to St. John's University basketball. Arlene and Nick have been married for a thousand years.

I lived around the corner from them. On this Sunday visit, Nick was out and she started discussing the alien, untrustworthy, chilling unfriendliness of the church of Rome at its worst.

"You have to write about these people. It is your job to expose them," she said.

"Me alone?"

"Yes. They are so bad that they must be exposed," she said. "You are the one who must do it. You're Irish," she said.

"The whole church is in Rome."

"The Irish run it here," she said.

"Rome starts it."

"The Irish finish it," she said.

"I still don't know about spreading scandal about the church," I said.

"I hadn't realized that you were so afraid," she said. "You spreading scandal? What about these priests and these liars, these bishops? When they molest a boy and act like it never happened. What are we supposed to do, keep our mouths shut? How do you ever make anything better by ignoring it?"

"I'll have to think," I said.

"Why? Just start doing it. It's your duty to tell people about this." She mentioned a friend of hers who is a nun.

"Do you know what she calls these priests? 'Toxic waste.' "

Right now she was holding the door open for me to walk into something that upbringing had made unthinkable. I would have to get ahold of my Aunt Harriet and see where she stood. She was out in Levittown, on Long Island, and I was in the center of Queens, which was inconvenient and left me more vulnerable to other opinions. Sure, you're vulnerable. This is the one biggest decision of my life. Breeding and blood can't be shucked off all at once.

I come out of the Queens County of the past, where the last parish is St. Camillus in Rockaway, a small white wooden building, dripping with seawater from the Atlantic Ocean, which is just up a short block. The Irish say proudly that the next parish is Knock, county Mayo. Which is as truthful as the tides of the ocean; the religion in Queens comes out of the gloomiest and most fearful of old Ireland.

At the same time, St. Camillus is the church that gave us so much hope and beauty in Maura Clarke, a Maryknoll nun who was one of four missionaries murdered at the airport in El Salvador by soldiers. But the Irish in Ireland, who are supposed to be so constricted sexually, to have cast temptations of the flesh into the cold sea, were involved in the sex scandals in the 1980s.

The Irish in Ireland, who crossed the ocean to run the church in America, live up beautifully to Arlene D'Arienzo's judgment.

First flash out of the gate came the photo of Bishop Eamonn Casey and Father Michael Cleary of the working-class town of Ballyfermott standing with the pope at a youth mass at the Galway racetrack. Cleary was in the picture with the pope because the pope was enthralled with him for the way he charged through the last trench in an attempt to stop even the talk of abortion and contraception in the wonderful nation: Cleary burst into a television studio with a squad of brain-handicapped children while a group of women favoring abortion were being interviewed. Cleary called upon God. The brain-handicapped children wandered among the camera cables. "Some of them were ga-ga," one of the women, writer Nell McCafferty, recalls.

But the pope photo caused a monsoon of delicious gossip. How can you store secrets anymore when the two of them are right out there posing with the pope and practically begging you to tell on them? When we know that: Bishop Casey screws a gorgeous woman, Annie Murphy, in the morning and then rushes off to confession and returns in the state of grace and just in time to say mass. It's a soaring experience. He then shucks off his vestments and again goes flying atop Annie Murphy.

Q. How do we know this to be true?

A. Because Annie Murphy put it all on paper.

There were also a few dollars missing from church accounts and the bishop moved out to Florida, to South America, and then England, where he lives now and yearns for the sight of Galway today, but has been told to stay in England where the likes of him belong.

The good priest who was with him on that momentous day with the pontiff, Father Cleary, also suffered an assault of the tongues. Prior to this, he was known locally as the Widow's Friend. Now the name danced across the country. He also was a member of a seven-voice group, the Singing Priests. Fine. And then one of the seven came up a pedophile and the Catholic church, which was supposed to run Ireland, collapsed.

On New Year's Eve 1995, the past came out of the kitchen wall and hit the father of Colm O'Gorman and caused him to break down.

All those years before, Colm O'Gorman, then seventeen, was in his kitchen putting down salt so the slugs wouldn't get in. Then he went upstairs and was abused by the houseguest, Father Sean Fortune. Colm came down and made tea. He said it was the only thing he could think of. He had been raped, but he couldn't admit that. It had to be an affair, he reasoned. Absolutely marvelous. The affair went on. Father Fortune then asked Colm to find him someone younger to sleep with. He'd pay for the pimping. Until then, Colm had thought he was the only one. Now he was just another piece of young meat and the guy wanted even younger. Spring lamb. Colm wound up sleeping in the streets of Dublin for several years.

And for all this time, for twelve years, his father, a deeply religious churchman, had tried to live in denial and confusion. But now on this New Year's Eve, with Colm suddenly in the house with a sister who had brought him home, the father fell apart.

Afterwards, the sister, Barbara, and Colm O'Gorman sat in the empty kitchen with a detective named Pat Mulcahy and Colm went over the rapes by Father Fortune.

"Mulcahy was amazing," O'Gorman said the other day. "He never put words in my mouth. He just let me say what I thought it was."

O'Gorman started it. Then more and more of Sean Fortune's victims came out. There were sixty-six counts. And four suicides. Then Father Fortune committed suicide. Bishop Comiskey, in charge of the area, hung up his shepherd's staff and trotted away as fast as his fat feet could carry him and was gone from church and countryside before parishioners could assault him. The church, once as much a part of Ireland as peat, began to collapse. Priests disappeared. In some parishes in the west of Ireland, which is empty to begin with, people took over the churches and said mass without the ceremony of consecrating the host.

There have been four great movements in modern America that occurred without the news reporting industry knowing anything about them until they became a part of regular life. The first was civil rights, then the women and, third, homosexuals and, last and suddenly, the crumbling of the Catholic church. You can blame the church's condition on the Irish, who gave us total religious insanity. They are a race that sat in the rain for a couple of thousand years and promoted the most crazed beliefs in personal living outside of the hillbillies. The symbol is Edward Egan, cardinal, archbishop, who lives amidst the best Irish lace curtains on Madison Avenue in Manhattan.

The first marvelous religious politician was Archbishop Hughes of New York, who told Lincoln that Catholics would "fight to the death" to save the union. But he assured his president that Catholics would do nothing to end slavery, which he found to be useful. Growing up, Hughes worked as an overseer for a slave crew and he said that it bothered him greatly. His brother-in-law, William Rodriguez, who got half the architect's fee for St. Patrick's Cathedral, came from a slaveholding family in Santo Domingo and preached the glory of free labor to Hughes. Suddenly, Hughes decided that slavery was legitimate. There also were slaves toiling in Catholic institutions in Baltimore. Bishops such as Peter Kenrick wept about slavery in public and personally owned slaves.

Irish Catholic publications were so bad—"ugly black niggers"— that the government closed them down. Rome never uttered a word. Through history, they always were afraid to offend Spain and Portugal, who adored slavery—the Catholic church never seems to be against any organized evil. With this as a heritage, the church spent two hundred years as America's worst racists. If John Kennedy had not arrived in 1960 to save Irish souls, the Irish Catholics would surely have been considered—and probably so right now—as aggressive South Africans.

Look at almost any Irish bishop or cardinal and you have most offensive behavior.

Thomas Daily, who as Bishop of Brooklyn lived big in Fort Greene in Brooklyn, was saved by the calendar and resigned at age seventy-five. When, in fair comment, he should have been indicted in two places—Boston and Brooklyn—for hiding and moving around dangerous pedophiles. Another was William Murphy of Long Island, and we will get to him later. All were blessed and boosted by Bernard Law, Cardinal of Boston, along with others such as McCormack in New Hampshire, O'Brien in Phoenix, McCarrick in Washington, D.C., Mahony of Los Angeles, and on through the green fields.

I don't know what they are in charge of. If they can't protect the neighbor's children from their own priests, then they have no ability to do anything but arrive early for dinner. Of course they should quit before the people finally understand it is their duty to throw them out.

These Irish brought Jansenism to the big cities of America. Jansenism is an inherited parasite that first appeared when the British ruled Ireland and closed all seminaries so that young Catholics who wanted to serve fled to France, where a priest, Cornelius Jansen, ran a seminary in the seventeenth century. Jansen was delirious over sins of the flesh. If you held a girl's hand, you died in hell. These poor repressed priests, frightened by the slightest urge, went back to Ireland and ran the religion of the nation. It was a doctrine so narrow that services should have been held in an alley. All these years later its followers are at least as grim. The symbol today is

Father Micheal Ledwith, president of the Irish national seminary, St. Patrick's in Maynooth, in the splendor of Kildare. It stands with James Joyce's words swirling about it. Ledwith ran a cold, disciplined, maddening religion, which was fine except seminarians complained that he kept unfolding his hands and pawing over seminarians. Although he has denied the charges against him, leave he must. He went to Seattle, to the Ramtha School of Enlightenment. This is a place where the founder channels to a thirty-five-thousand-year-old warrior. Through the rains, too.

His kind of Irish made sex with women a secret act, the act of darkness. The Sixth Commandment. Thou Shall Not Commit Adultery. "That's the mortler!" my friend Donal Donnelly cries. Through a millennium, maybe most of a second millennium, Jansenism stayed the hands of Catholics. If the loins are warming, go to confession. They demanded so unceasingly that people live a cold life that a church so constricted would writhe uncontrollably and so many would decide that if women are so bad, then it might be best to sleep with a choirboy. When the public today understood what was going on, they exploded. There was no question that priests got into virtually no trouble because of being with women of any age, but were candidates for execution because of boys. And for the first time ever, the bishops and cardinals, always so saintly, now were looked at as suspects.

What is it that these bishops and cardinals actually do for their daily bread? Christ has said, in one of the lines from the Gospels that I believe in my heart, "Woe is to he who does harm to a child. It is better that he ties a millstone around his neck and jumps off a cliff."

And by failing to take any action, these regents are nothing more than stuffy accomplices in molesting children. Some have been personally involved in abuse. Others have stonewalled investigations and moved pedophiles from one parish to another. Listen to one of them explain:

Edward Egan. Cardinal, archbishop of New York, residing at St. Patrick's Cathedral, is giving a deposition in Bridgeport, Connecticut, where he was assigned before moving to New York. In this deposition, Egan is answering questions under oath about priests sexually abusing altar boys. Egan is being questioned by Cindy Robinson, a Bridgeport attorney, who represents a young man who reported that he was sexually abused by a priest.

Q. (Lawyer Cindy Robinson for plaintiff) He admits apparently that he had oral sex with this young boy and that he actually bit his penis to prevent ejaculation. He advised the boy to go to confession elsewhere.

A. (Egan) Well, I think you're not exactly right . . . It seemed to me that the gentleman in question was an eighteen-year-old student at Sacred Heart University.

Q. Are you aware of the fact that in December of 1964 that an individual under twenty-one years of age was a minor in the state of Connecticut?

A. My problem, my clarification had to do with the expression, "a young boy" about an eighteen-year-old.

Q. A young—all right, a minor, is that better then?

A. Fine.

He isn't acting like a cardinal, an archbishop; he is a cheap criminal lawyer trying to get somebody off on a sodomy charge by saying he didn't do it because his zipper was stuck.

Q. What do you think is the responsibility of your diocese?

A. I think that perhaps there is none. A priest actually is a contractor for the diocese. He is self-employed. Therefore, the priest is liable but as he is an individual and not part of the diocese then he is personally responsible, but not the diocese.

Q. Even in the case of Father Brett, who is charged with molesting children?

A. I do not see it as the responsibility of the diocese.

He is supposed to lead us and instead he finds these tiny devious arguments. He speaks in a swirl of irrelevancies. "A minor." He had paid money in secret to at least one priest in order to have him refrain from admitting anything at a trial of a victim. It was called "hush money" in *The Hartford Courant*. When the court announced it was going to allow testimony about the money, Egan settled the case the next day.

The Irish are supposed to be a people who resent authority, yet the truth is that one cocked eyebrow from a priest and a town falls to its knees. They were taught in Ireland by a deplorable figure, Cardinal Paul Cullen, who said the great famine of 1845 was "a calamity with which God wishes to purify the Irish people." His life was chinaware and candles and other people's money. He dismissed the peasants dying in the fields as mere happenstance.

The people came to New York with this gloomy obedience and it has lasted through the generations with so many families. Many of the Fighting Irish were actually the Genuflecting Irish. They could fight in a war valiantly, but in conflicts in life, day in and day out, one year after the other, the inclination to bow to authority prevailed without thought, which was the center of the religion; let the priest do the thinking.

Because of their church, the Irish think less and boast more than any race ever to hit the ground.

The Irish used movies to take over the religion in America, and to make enormous changes in the country's culture. There were fifteen hundred movies made about priests, worldwide, between 1942 and just yesterday. However, the Irish blood demanded that they practice backbiting and slander as a daily practice and it always was about the Jews running the movies. Which it seems that the Jews did. Irish marketing skills were for anything in a bottle, or policy, or knitware. The Jews sold movies. The studios were owned by Louis B. Mayer, Sam Goldwyn, the Warner brothers, David Selznick, Harry Cohen,

Adolph Zukor. They used miles of film for Catholic movies because they could make money with them, and therefore did all you could hope for from any group, Catholics included. This completely eluded the Catholics. How can you hate anybody if you realize that they don't give you anything to hate? In the thirties Cardinal Dougherty of Philadelphia, with a cold eye on Jewish studios, tried to censor everything that you could see. He made it a sin for anybody to even walk into a movie house if it showed a banned movie. For a time this had a dramatic effect on the box offices, although it could not last. In 1933, the Catholic bishops had a man named John Cantwell, who shrieked about "Jews" and "Pagans" running Hollywood. Absolutely marvelous! The Catholics also presented one Joseph Breen as the ruler of all of movies. The film studios gave the impression that whatever Breen said would be in their scripts. It was nonsense, but the church lived in illusion, and the movie people helped them do so.

The church frauds didn't know what they were looking at. Their sinister, controlling Jewish studio heads put out so many saccharine movies about Catholics that they might as well have used big churches as sound studios. Bing Crosby's *Going My Way* was at once the holiest and most popular movie. From the movie Crosby also had huge single recordings of "Going My Way" and "Swinging On a Star." I don't even know the name of the priest Crosby played, but for the rest of his life, Bing Crosby was a famous priest. Also in *Going My Way* was Barry Fitzgerald, who had a music box attached to a bottle of whisky, but for use only for times like Christmas. When he opened the box, it played "Too-Ra-Loo-Ra-Loo-Ral" and Crosby made that a big record, the third from the one picture. Crosby was the same priest in *The Bells of St. Mary's* and Crosby again recorded the song and much of a nation listened. Actor Frank McHugh also turned his collar around for the movie. McHugh rarely got back into a straight collar. He became Father Timothy O'Dowd in a couple of movies, and to all headwaiters.

Still, today, there are people like Harry Haun of *Playbill* magazine, who remember them title for title. Pat O'Brien was Father Duffy in *The Fighting 69th* and then *Fighting Father Dunne* and *The Fireball,* Father O'Hara. O'Brien was a priest and James Cagney a hoodlum in *Angels with Dirty Faces,* which was the gangster movie of my time. They had grown up in the same neighborhood. James Cagney, as bad guy Rocky, asks Pat O'Brien as Father Jerry, how he decided to become a priest. The priest says he got the idea when he was riding on the top of a bus that passed St. Patrick's Cathedral. Bad Boy Rocky answers, "That's funny. I got an idea on top of a bus one time. Got me six years."

Spencer Tracy was Father Flanagan of *Boys Town.* In *Men of Boys Town,* he lifted us right out of the streets into a stamping, roaring joy. A reform school superintendent told Tracy that he was not going to be allowed to see anybody because he was a priest and if he took off that collar he would show it to him. Slowly, elegantly, Tracy reached up, craned his neck as I recall, and pulled the collar out of his shirt. We nearly fainted with excitement. What he did to the guy was anticlimactic. Took the reform school guy by the throat and made him say yes. That was all right. But the collar was the whole thing. The movie house, the Jerome, now is a factory of some kind, but in the emptiness of a Saturday afternoon you can hear our cheering. Gregory Peck played Father Francis Chisholm in *The Keys of the Kingdom.* My friend Donal Donnelly was Archbishop Gildea in *Godfather III.*

Catholics had the thrill of recognition. No matter what the religion, however, people paid to see the mysticism of movies about nuns. Perhaps the actresses weren't pure Irish, but they were in a run started by Pat O'Brien's brogue. In *The Nun's Story,* the last scene they shot had Audrey Hepburn leaving the convent for good with a glorious choir touching the sky. Director Fred Zimmerman took the music out. He said it would make it seem as if she were elated to be leaving the church. Great actresses put on habits: Deborah Kerr was in *Heaven Knows, Mr. Allison* and Lilia Skala was opposite Sidney Poitier in *Lilies of the Field.* Rosalind Russell was a mother superior, Peggy Wood was in *The Sound of Music,* and Jennifer Jones won an Oscar for *The Song of Bernadette.* Whoopi Goldberg was in two straight *Sister*s films.

As late as the eighties, they were movies you could make money with. Still, the blind Irish backbiting did not stop. By now, it was obvious that for decades they were beside themselves with jealousy of the Jews. It didn't matter what the movies were about. I remember being in about the seventh grade standing in church on Sunday while the priest asked everybody to take the Oath of the Legion of Decency, which labeled films as unobjectionable or objectionable. We couldn't look at each other because it would cause you to laugh out loud. Whatever was on the objectionable list was the first movie we were going to see. I remember the priests were uncontrollable over a movie in the fifties called *The Moon Is Blue* and I went to see it twice because I thought I missed the dirty part.

And now, I had Arlene D'Arienzo telling me that I had an obligation to attack the church, and I knew that she was right about the Irish.

I almost had the incentive shattered before I started. This happened when I went to see my friend Mike Dowd, the lawyer. I knew he was starting to represent victims of abuse by the church. Now his office is on Fifth Avenue. We both come out of the past on Queens Boulevard.

"Let me tell you what I've been doing," he said. "A woman in Throgs Neck named O'Rourke calls me and says that her son had been abused by the church and she wants to talk to me. So I went up there the other afternoon . . ."

Right away, he started taking me into the darkest alley:

"She brings in her son. He's nineteen now. She and her husband leave the room because they get too embarrassed when the son talks.

The son starts telling me he was twelve and in grammar school when he has this nun bringing him coffee, a bagel, and a *Daily News* in school every morning. Then she had him over to her house in the afternoons. First with other kids. Then one day she has him there alone."

I flinch, but Mike doesn't even pause. "They were on the floor playing a board game of some kind and she took his head and pushed it under her skirt . . ."

I guess I blinked. I don't know. Mike and I have talked about murder and mayhem. But this pushed me back.

". . . Fifty or sixty times in the afternoons."

He shrugged. "I asked the lawyer for the archdiocese if they wanted to settle quietly. Why, of course they would. Zero is the number. The diocesan lawyer tried to justify a lower payment by painting the family as dysfunctional. I said to him, 'Isn't it true that the most vulnerable children to sexual assaults are from a family like this? A jury might think this showed how vulnerable the twelve-year-old was.' Do you know what the lawyer said? That I was suing because I spent so many years in Catholic schools that I must hate the church. What is it, first grade to law diploma, nineteen years? I told him we would leave that to the jury.

"We went through four witnesses. Then I happened to mention to these geniuses from the archdiocese, 'You know who was in charge of diocesan education when this went on, don't you? The records show Bishop Edward Egan. My question to you is, 'Will he get his red hat after four or five hours of my cross examining?' "

The church settled by dusk. Mike Dowd has a copy of the check in his desk. The archdiocese's crest is in one corner. The amount is $1,550,000.

At first, this business of taking money from God seemed to be a rash act, a deliberate throwing of yourself into the fires forever. Then the vision of the courtroom drifted through my mind. A room

in the old Manhattan Civil Court courthouse, a legal slum. There
was a pillar in the center of the room that if a bad moment suddenly
swooped in, a lawyer could hide behind the pillar and not be seen by
the jury, which then might forget the evil moment. It is a place
where nothing is sacred. Why, then, cringe if even the Catholic
church stirs the dust of the room by being there for the same grubby
business as anybody else?

I walked from Dowd's office to Penn Station. I was thinking of
riding out to Long Island to talk with my aunt. But she was in Sara-
sota, Florida, at her nephew's house. I took the first train out to
Woodside, which is ten minutes away, through the tunnel under the
river. The train comes out looking over the Sunnyside yards, once
the largest passenger car yards in the country. Woodside is part of
both Dowd's and my upbringing. When my father and mother failed
to keep pace with the landlord in an apartment over in Woodside,
they moved back into my grandmother's two-story frame house on
101st Avenue in Richmond Hill. Very soon, my father was gone. After
which I went through grammar school pretending he was dead. I also
believed that he would go to hell because of that. I was tormented by
my mother, who didn't go near church. She was taunting hell. Three
blocks up the side street from the house on 101st Avenue was the
main yard for the Long Island Railroad. The steam locomotives were
packed together like logs in a river. These big black bellies filled the
air with soot. They darkened the sky with clouds that blew across the
neighborhoods, dripping wet soot that ruined the wash on lines. Bad
weather was a challenge to housewives. But the steam locomotives
had none of nature's excitement and grace. They let off steam at four
in the afternoon. One day the big neighborhood football game at the
playground across from the engine yards went too late, and the Dun-
ton Maroons' A. J. Pryor, the only person in Queens ever to have initials for a first name, disappeared into a cloud bank and when he
came out he was in the end zone with the winning touchdown.

The ride on the railroad this day caused another wartime night on 101st Avenue to come back to me as if it were last week.

That was the Sunday night I carried that suitcase over to Penn Station for a train to Tullahoma, Tennessee, where Peter was in armored training at Camp Forrest. The coach car was old and smelled of railroad smoke. I put the suitcase up on the rack; my Aunt Harriet arranged herself in the coach seat with a book on her lap and rosary beads in her hands. I banged on the smeared window as her car slid past me. Harriet traveled with her prayers, her love for her husband, and the hopes of getting a job in a town she had never heard of until a few days ago. She rented a room in a large house alongside the railroad tracks in Tullahoma. She went to a department store, Miller Brothers of Chattanooga, and told them with a believable young face that she had worked in Macy's for ten years. That would have made her about age nine when she began at Macy's. The manager, Mr. White, was elated. You sure don't often get someone down here who worked in Macy's in New York. "We don't even know people who have shopped in Macy's," he said.

She remembers her salary was so low, forty cents an hour, and her room rent so high—the landlady disliked soldiers and charged them all she could—that she had to ask for money from home to pay the rent. All day, she heard the customers talking about how they hated soldiers and their families. A sign in the store bathroom said, DO NOT COMB HARE OVER BASIN. The sign was there for as long as she was. She cites it today because of her great disdain for improper language.

There was no Catholic church in Tullahoma. Once a week an itinerant priest came through town and said mass at a local hall, the name of which she can't remember. She spent many nights in her room with a radio that had a couple of hillbilly stations and her books and her prayers. "Prayer got me through Tennessee," she says.

Her husband then was shipped to Camp Kilmer, New Jersey, an

embarkation camp. Again, she came home with her suitcase. It was as clear as a rifle shot that he would be shipped overseas any day, and he was.

She spent the next couple of years working on Wall Street. She came home every night to 101st Avenue and in the front hall grabbed the small envelope called V-Mail with her husband's letter inside, and ran upstairs and read it a hundred times in her room.

There was a Saturday morning when my Uncle Jim and I were downstairs and Harriet was up in her room and a Western Union messenger came to the door with a telegram in Harriet's name that had the red star of the War Department.

Harriet came down the stairs calmly.

"Do you want me to open it?" my Uncle Jim said.

"Sure," Harriet said.

Then he opened it. Or he tried to. His hands shook.

"It's all right. Just open it," she said.

She showed no sign of distress. Her prayers and the life she had led calmed her and left her in the state of grace. She had loved every day in her religion; it had given her something to lean on. Which is what she had now. She needed no banister on the staircase. She was sure that the telegram would not say that her husband had been killed. She was sure that he was hurt. That would be good. It would keep him out of more battles where he could get killed.

Finally, her brother got the telegram open. The words were typed in purple capitals and pasted in strips on the yellow page.

"Your husband, Private Peter J. Arnone, has been wounded in action in the European Theater of Operations. Letter to follow. Ulio. The Adjutant General."

She threw the telegram away. She was not much for saving mementos of the war that took her husband away for over five years.

Chapter Five

Always, I went around seeing my own movie in my mind, a big lifelike close-up of a priest walking under the trees in Richmond Hill with his hand inside his tunic, on the way to care for the sick. Real was another thing. There was the day when I bumped into Father Roesch, the pastor of Our Lady Queen of Martyrs church on Queens Boulevard, and he asked me if I wanted to come to a small dinner he was having for Father Bruce Ritter, who at that time was considered the priest closest to God. The church was a light tan fieldstone fortress on the corner of Queens Boulevard in Forest Hills. It had great big good collections and donations, and Ritter was coming out to meet the parish people who put up money. When Ritter met someone with money he stood alongside them so closely and for so long that he seemed to be cemented to them.

He ran Covenant House on Tenth Avenue in Manhattan, his home for poor and helpless young girls and boys in Times Square. He said he was a true saint because his first success in Covenant House came when he took in six kids, four boys and two girls, on a cold December night in 1969. He spoke street talk. "Took in six, man, saved two, man." One of the saved called himself Sergeant Pepper. Ritter said he also saved all these fourteen-year-old girls from poorest Duluth who were found selling themselves on one stretch of Times Square sidewalk, the Minnesota Strip.

I knew one thing. Almost every young woman out there on the turf, as we called it, was of color and from uptown or Brooklyn. I saw no palefaces who had stepped out of Minnesota snow. I give myself that tiny bit of credit for recognizing that.

I didn't go to the dinner. I didn't give a reason. When I don't do something and don't know why, it usually turns out that I had a reason inside me that I didn't even know about at the time.

In this case, my friend Michael Daly of the *Daily News* newspaper had told me, "Jack Maple says kids tell him that Ritter is a chicken hawk."

Maple was a transit cop who worked Times Square, and who would become the deputy commissioner who started the program known as Compstat, which is credited with bringing down crime wherever it is used. The phrase *chicken hawk* was too disturbing for me to grasp. I let the subject pass by me like paper blowing in the gutter. Or I thought I had. Every time I saw Ritter's name, I had doubt running into suspicion. I better start walking Times Square, I told myself.

Then I am watching Ronald Reagan in his state of the union speech calling out Ritter's name as a hero to a crash of applause. Soon, Ritter was the Person of the Week on ABC News, a hero on *60 Minutes,* a thrilling expert on the *Today* show.

These were his credentials. What did I have to throw at him? He was a priest. I had a rumor.

It turned out that I wasn't the only one who didn't grasp the situation right away. "I was the lieutenant in Times Square and I didn't know anything at first," Ray Kelly was saying one night. He now is the city's police commissioner. "We'd go to Ritter and say, 'Can you give us some names of these girls so we can try to contact their parents?' He waves his arm and says, 'Oh, man, they're everywhere.' Then he talks about himself. We never got the name of a single girl."

When the truth came out, it developed that on that first night he was saved by Covenant House, the boy known as Sergeant Pepper was sexually abused by Ritter. It never stopped. Later, Pepper wandered into the night unable to know who he was or what he was. I don't know where he is now.

And on the West Side of Manhattan, young boys climbed in and out of parked trailer trucks to sell themselves to men arriving in cars, and sometimes to Ritter himself.

Charles Sennott of *The Boston Globe* worked on the *New York Post* at that time, and he had the anger to write the first true story. Right away, all these rich sycophants around Ritter threatened Sennott. He immediately wrote another story. The rich people evaporated. Ritter tried one press conference. "He looks at me with these watery blue eyes and expects me to dissolve," Charlie says. "I went back and wrote another story. That makes the guy disappear." Sennott had done his job. I had not done mine. Ritter was through. He moved upstate and died.

Once, it was unthinkable to write of a priest in any tone except lovingly, and mildly humorous, particularly about a priest at the racetrack. You could not envision writing or discussing a priest's sexual attack on the young. But when the victims cried and people reported this, it was still considered scandalous and sinful to put such dark stories in a newspaper. For so long, only a few could understand that my business is to write a newspaper column three times a week, and in the years 2003 and 2004—not the thirties. I pay my rent. I am obligated to write about something such as this, of enormous importance, in order to inform people. What if I announced to my office, "I can't write about the church because I'm a Catholic and I should help them through this by keeping quiet"? The answer would be, "Go join a monastery."

In my old Forest Hills neighborhood, between my daughter Kelly and a curiosity that was finally being used, I found several former altar boys who came forward with allegations that they were sexually abused in the years from 1981 to 1983 by two priests in Queen of Martyrs. It has taken the old altar boys all these years to shuck off the humiliation and understand what happened and why they kept it hidden even to themselves. I had lived here for so many years, in a place where the young were absolutely safe and if anything, overprotected—that's exactly what we believed.

The mother of the three Davis boys was so obedient to her church that the priests were sure they could make her forget the matter with a note.

2-20-83
OUR LADY QUEEN OF MARTYRS RECTORY
110-06 QUEENS BOULEVARD
FOREST HILLS, N.Y. 11375

Dear Mrs. Davis,

In consequences of my conversation with the pastor, I write this brief note.

To say the least, I am ashamed and I am sorry—both for you and for Tommy. I had previously apologized to Tommy for my indiscretion.

The farthest thing on my mind would be ever to hurt Tommy. However, I have hurt him, and I am sorry.

I'm ashamed of my stupidity of my indiscretion for which I have no excuse, nor did I have any devious motive.

I hope you will both excuse and forgive me, and I pray that Tommy will, as well.

Sincerely,
Rev. Joseph P. Collins

The boy would get over the attack. Why wouldn't he? He isn't even twelve yet. Send him to a movie and he won't even know what happened. Send the woman a nice note. She won't be mad anymore.

On this day in the summer of 2002, I am walking on Queens Boulevard, truly the boulevard of broken dreams, on my way to the criminal courthouse to witness a ceremony of my church, the arraignment of a priest on charges of sexually assaulting a young boy. The sidewalk growls with the footsteps of defendants with court dates, lawyers wishing to get paid, and witnesses and jurors coerced by subpoenas. On the arraignment calendar on the first floor wall was the name of Peter Kiarie. His arraignment was called for mid-morning in a windowless room on the ground floor. Kiarie, forty-one, is a missionary priest from Africa, and a member of the Holy Ghost Fathers from France. The order has living quarters in Long Island City and Kiarie had arranged to say mass and preach at Blessed Virgin Mary Help of Christians church in Woodside. We always knew it as St. Mary's of Winfield, and it was famous for having pastors who were fascists.

This court appearance today would give the first real idea of whether the church was going to let civil authorities apprehend their perpetrators, for they always stopped the police and courts in Queens County. Once, a day like this would be unthinkable; who are you with your grubby police badge to even look at a priest? Just wait for a small moment until I can get the mayor down here and throw you out of your job. Pass on, priest.

I expected this because of a morning spent on the corner of Park Avenue and 50th Street in the fall of 1965. Politicians from all over the universe arrived for a United Nations assembly. We had the pope of Rome and President Lyndon Baines Johnson staying in the Waldorf-Astoria Towers, which is why I'm on the corner. Upstairs, Johnson said to presidential assistants Bill Moyers and Harold

Pachios: "I'd sure like to have my picture taken with the pope out on the street." When Lyndon Johnson says, I'd sure like, he means do it or you're dead.

So now they are on the sidewalk outside the Towers entrance on 50th Street, talking to Phil Walsh, chief of New York detectives, who was in charge of handling the pope.

Moyers was Texas Baptist to the point of being a minister. Pachios was Maine, good Greek Orthodox. Walsh was Flatbush Irish Roman Catholic.

"It's just one quick picture of the president and the pope," Pachios said. He was showing Walsh where they would have the cameras, across the street, along the wall of St. Bartholomew's, the big-money Episcopalian church. And Johnson would be here and the pope right at his side.

Today, I can still see Phil Walsh. Short. A fedora and glasses, the voice raspy.

"Listen. When His Holiness and that other fella come out here . . ."

Pachios and Moyers shrugged in defeat. "We're in the wrong city," Pachios said. There was no picture.

After speculating on whether the church would walk into the Queens court on this day and display the hammer, the other question was how could a Kenyan, a black, become a priest in France and wind up in Long Island City, Queens, in a dingy brick house on a side street, and from here travel the country to raise money for his order of missionaries? It is evidence of either the total chaos of the church or the most meticulous planning and operations seen since Alexander the Great. My money is on chaos.

The courtroom was so crowded I saw no seat at first. I was sure the place was packed for the priest but then when I looked around I saw that there were no Roman collars or flat Irish faces, or women with rosary beads.

A man in the last row had a little girl with her head in his lap and her legs sprawled. I squeezed past the man and sat on the edge of the bench with the little girl's legs behind me. I did the best I could not to bother her, but doesn't the kid stir and cause the father to snort. Then the little girl shifted and had her legs drawn up, her head buried in her father's lap and the first deep snores coming from her.

The father smiled. "She was asleep on my shoulder coming in here."

The priest could be any case now. First through the door from the detention pens came two young guys charged with arson of a 1989 Plymouth. One lawyer said that his client had been arrested inside his home at five in the morning. His sister was pregnant and had been up most of the night and therefore could testify that the young man never left the house. Still, the judge set one bail of $7,500 and the other of $5,000. Those sums would not be enough to keep a cocker spaniel from running away. The only reason for bail is to ensure that the defendant will appear for the next court date. Roots in the community should do it.

Now into the courtroom came a man in a light blue polo shirt. He was on probation for busting up his wife during a couple of family differences and there were orders of protection which he violated. In the row in front of me, a young woman in a sleeveless white top and with hair pulled back, leaned forward. She appeared to be somehow mixed up with the matter. The judge said the bail was $15,000. The defendant looked at the young woman. His mouth formed the words, "Do you have it?"

She said to him, silently, "I don't."

She was being asked for $15,000 in Queens, which is huge.

The judge set $1,000 bail in the next case. The lawyer turned to the family and with inquiring eyebrows held up one finger. The family sitting off to my right shook their heads.

Now in walked a young woman, twenty-five maybe, with her

light hair in a ponytail, and three young men, all in white polo shirts and black pants. They were charged with disorderly conduct in an empty lot alongside 97-48 Bristol Avenue in Ozone Park. Nativity parish. They all were let go.

I thought about days when any priest from Nativity parish could have seen that the matter never reached court.

Now look at where we are, waiting for a priest to come out of a detention pen.

He walked through the door from the pens. He was slim, with the usual color of defendants, black, and in a white polo shirt. Nobody announced that he was a Roman Catholic priest. He was charged with sexually assaulting a twelve-year-old boy on a Father's Day outing at Rockaway Beach. The priest was here from Africa for only a couple of weeks.

The priest appeared to pick out the precise trail of the pedophiles and child molesters. He became instantly friendly with the boy's mother, who worked in the church office. She was a single mother and welcomed a man, a priest, who was kind to her son. What could be more comforting than having a priest take the boy out on Father's Day?

The charges said that the assaults were in a grocery store, on the boardwalk on 116th Street, in a restaurant and on the bus coming home. I flinched. I spent the first third of my life on 116th Street.

The priest was up in front, silent and motionless. The judge set bail at $50,000. A court officer gave the priest a sheet of paper about the charges. He was reading it as he walked through the door into the detention pens. Nobody regarded him as an extraordinary defendant. The old power that would have settled this with a phone call was gone. Today, their arrests can become common and boring.

Later, a priest standing at the doors to St. Mary's in Woodside said, in a heavy Irish accent, "We never should have had the woman here. She was a welfare case. Disturbed woman. We took her in. I think you'll find that he is innocent." His tone put reasonable doubt in my mind. Some weeks later, a jury would take four hours to find the priest not guilty. He went outside and sat on a bench and buried his face in his hands. Then he got up and went to the clerk's office to have his passport returned. He left the court ready to fly back to Kenya. And he left in all observers, including this keenest of all, the reminder that once again, from the Constitution on, a not guilty is a possibility every time out, and all reporting should reflect this. The only place where nothing is in doubt is the cemetery.

Chapter Six

By noon, streaks of sun rippled across the only empty field I've ever seen in a cemetery. It was as if all the dead had come out of the ground in their shrouds and walked away. I am in the center of the Catholic church's beliefs, a cemetery, and I am intensely interested in these three acres or so in the corner of St. Michael's Cemetery on Astoria Boulevard in the heart of Queens. This part of the cemetery has one headstone in the center and a couple of old gray broken stone stumps sticking out of the grass like an old man's last teeth. Otherwise it is an empty field.

I thought right away that this would be a terrific Previously Owned cemetery. I could get enough people together to purchase the disappeared graves as secondhand lots. This could break the hold that the organized church has over ground for which they pay not a dollar in taxes.

The cemetery proves that death is endless. It starts on the day you are born and asserts the only true power on earth, the passing, burial, and from then on the misuse of time, the visits to the gravesite that end as families die, and the friends are gone and the gravemarkers wither and crumble and there are no visitors and nothing to visit. Whoever they were, they are beyond the grave. Nothing is left in the grave. Worms win.

All this vacant ground is surrounded by regular rows of graves, and as you walk over this empty stretch, the ground gives too much, moaning that it is hollow, that there is nothing left in the graves. If there is nothing there, are they still graves?

Only one headstone shows here in this corner of St. Michael's because the cemetery, started in 1852, originally was a place for the poor. The first dead were buried in a churchyard at St. Michael's church on 99th Street on the West Side in Manhattan. When that became overcrowded they moved the cemetery to Queens. Nobody had money for a gravestone that would last against weather coming from the Atlantic. The families used a wood cross, a piece of limestone, porous and practically dissolving from moisture, or plain cement. The families to follow could buy granite tombstones.

The cemetery office has old books filled with exquisite penmanship on the records of the dead and their gravesites. They left a record that has lasted 150 years and should go longer. There is the name, date of death, and location of grave. Many show that there isn't a tenth cousin alive to claim ownership.

That gave me my first thought. I could pay the cemetery for ownership of this disappeared grave. The church is so maimed by the sex scandal that a little bribery doesn't count.

The church terms it sacred ground. A Catholic cemetery is made sacred by a rite that is maybe fifteen hundred years old. The church is demented on death. There is a heritage of a special rite, consecratio cymiterii, which calls for taking five wooden crosses and placing one at the center and the others at the four points of the compass. The bishop gets in the center and holds high a stick filled with water and then the bishop whirls like a lawn sprinkler. Holy water flies into the air. He recites long prayers identical with an eighth-century rite. Candles are lit, incense is spread, then all proceed to church, where solemn mass is celebrated. As they kneel in church, this great doused ground outside shines with holiness. It is now sacred.

This is part of the mysticism of the Catholic church that produces much suspicion and minimal belief as some ancient law of the church is found to be a fake and a fraud. Rome forced people to take an oath against such modernism. After the church dogged it with Hitler, and that is the best you can say for them, the excuse was that Communism was worse. Too many Catholics in all countries rejected the stand against modernism. If the last church didn't want to fight Hitler, then we might as well get another church. But right away, Rome barred all suggestions of modernism, the most threatening being the new role of women. They create all the fear about everything.

The Catholic church has been in first place because of the dead. You have the cemeteries it owns. People beg the pastor for a plot in sacred ground for their aunt. That's why Catholics have been in first place.

Once excited Catholics went to the late Joseph Mugavero, the best bishop of Brooklyn we've had, and one was saying, "Bishop, you've got to do something. All we see is Falwell, Falwell, Falwell on television. Why can't we go on television and at least compete with the guy?"

Mugavero asked quietly, "How many acres does Falwell have?"

"None," somebody said.

"Then what are we talking about?" Mugavero said, holding out his hands.

Jerry Falwell can't even bury your dog.

If the church doesn't sell me plots, I will try the large Lutheran and Jewish cemeteries in my area.

Suddenly, as I write I am interrupted. "Why are you saying that Mugavero was the best bishop?" my daughter Rosemary says. She says this as I write and this is why this book is so torturous to do. Not just because of her. Every phone call from victims and their families interrupts your whole life. This time my daughter has a printout of what I am writing in her hands and she is complaining.

"He was such a good bishop he wanted ten thousand for an annulment."

Her husband, Tony Dunne, had married a woman when they were both young and it didn't last. He and my daughter wanted to marry in a Catholic church ceremony, but the church doesn't marry anybody divorced. Only an annulment gets you to the altar. An annulment is purchased.

"And the ten thousand was nothing," she said. "That's only money. What they wanted was for Tony and his first wife to send letters saying that they had not talked about having children before they were married and then afterwards she refused to have any. They wanted Tony to lie. Then they wanted him to get the former wife to lie. After you get these lies, you put ten thousand with them and you get an annulment. That says the marriage never happened. If you put up twenty thousand, they'll say that you never even knew the woman."

"How are you so sure?"

"Because I was involved."

"Who was the money supposed to go to?"

"The bishop. What are you, crazy? Never mind ten thousand. The lies. They said you had to lie."

"Why didn't you ever tell me?"

"Because it was my business and you would have written about it and gone on to something else and left us in turmoil. Your business was to pay for the wedding."

"What do you want me to do?"

"Take out where you say he's the best bishop."

Dealing with the Catholic church on the dead is cheaper and simpler. You must pay for the prayers and plot. If it were possible to annul a person's entire life and replace it with a gleaming white commendation, there would be no such thing as an inheritance. All money from all lifetimes would go to the churchman who signs the pass to heaven. If people in Queens dream, it is about that. For it seems like every dead body in the east is buried in Queens. The borough now has about 4.5 dead bodies to every person who is purportedly alive. If you think of your dear departed, it always is with the hope and prayer that the person made it all the way, higher than the stars, to heaven.

Our prayers for the dead, like the rest of the church droning, are almost as lifeless as the body you pray for. Starting with prayers for the dead, I would like to then go on and try meaningful language for life today in the Catholic religion. God knows who he is, and all praise and honor is given with such repetition that so many people cannot be anything but inattentive and bored.

Eulogies are at best uninformed and boring. The priests who give them don't know anything about the dead person. The words over the casket are dreadfully boring. At their hour of death, the departing are yawned at.

How did they travel through life? What did they do to feed their families? Through all those young years, Christ worked as an obscure carpenter. Don't celebrate only carpentry. He worked. Think of that as an example as you pray for the dead. It might be the only real thing said about them. What did they do for a living?

Oh, Lord, a carpenter and son of a carpenter.
Cover us in sawdust.
Soak us in sweat.
Bless our Jobs.
Let our hands become a novena.
To let our work spread new Jobs to the jobless.

Knowing that a father who works can look at his son.

That a mother who works revels in the wonders of her efforts. Her roof.
*   The clothes and food for her children.*

Let our concentration become a benediction.

For we teach reading to a child

Whose eyes now see through the mists to a future.

Bless our Jobs.

By our work help those rebuffed by life.

The elation at assisting.

Let us understand that scorning the poor is to taunt Christ crucified.

Oh, Lord, with your hand, we answer all alarms.

Let us be the ambulance.

Because we work, we walk in dignity and we bring all others. Our heads
*   bow only for you, Oh, Lord.*

Every day, we forgive our trespasses as we forgive those who trespass
*   against us. Amen.*

The present rites of death and burial have turned Catholic church Catholicism into a last breath religion. That is why there are no ex-Catholics. Once vaccinated with the church religion, it lasts through all the years. You can ignore, deny, evade. Then let there be one twinge in the chest, one suddenly missed breath, and there still is this sudden begging for a priest. They'll take the odd doctor if one happens along, but first they want to clutch a cross and have the priest give extreme unction, or whatever it is called now. It has been downgraded from a sacrament to simply *anointing*.

This final fear should be hurled out of our lives. The priest is not going to save your soul. Nor is the building he patrols, no matter the grandeur and glory of it. You save yourself by honest work in the name of God and of the dead generations who have gone before us and from whom we derive our legacy of compassion, of never being indifferent to suffering of others. An important part of the Catholic religion is to always say something nice to somebody. If you want to save your soul, try that. It is one of the dictums that shows the difference between the failed church of Rome, and the American religion I believe in.

Once, at a luncheon of the New York Patrolmen's Benevolent Association, the chaplain, Msgr. John Kowsky, cried out that the governor of the state, at the time it was Mario Cuomo, must sign a death penalty bill into law. Cuomo believed life and death was God's property and not ours.

Kowsky prayed aloud, "For our governor, just one little thing he's got to do, Lord: Learn to turn the switch."

At that moment, that man was trying to stand between God and me. I believe in God more deeply than ever and in the love of all neighbors. What church allows its people to demand death?

After St. Michael's, I went to Cypress Hills cemetery, which is secular, a great part of it a national cemetery. One end, however, was private grounds. In the corner was a ten-story hill with gravestones on it. It was some hike to the top. Sitting in front of one headstone with the name MELVIN MENDOZA was the brother, Angel Mendoza. The deceased lived and was shot dead on the streets. He always said he wanted to be on top of the world. Therefore, the brother bought him this spot, so he could see to the downtown buildings of Manhattan, dominated by the World Trade Center towers. Then a Chinese undertaker inspecting the place put his foot under the ground and struck a buried refrigerator. Soon it was found that the whole hill consisted of a layer of dirt covering a junk heap. Most people ran to the courts. Angel Mendoza wouldn't move. They offered to disinter the body and plant it at a nicer place. He said no.

That time, high in the hazy sky of Manhattan, were the Twin

Towers. If he looked the other way, he saw the waters of Jamaica Bay as they ran into the Atlantic Ocean. Underneath his brother's grave was a mountain of refuse, tires, carpet strips, auto parts, anything. Angel didn't care. His brother was on top of the world. On September 11 of '01, the Trade Center disappeared. The brother had the grave moved.

Chapter Seven

A psychiatrist I know well, Dr. Paula Eagle, called and said that she had a patient, who also was a doctor, who wanted to tell people about what had happened to her. Paula thought it was something she had never heard before.

The patient was Diana Williamson, and I met her on the stoop of Paula Eagle's townhouse on East 36th Street, which was the first building in a long time that had a story for me that was below the fifth or sixth floor walkup.

Diana Williamson was just back from an international conference on AIDS. For me, she has been remembering scenes, and parts of them, of being age six and being raped and sodomized in school many times by a priest in Massachusetts, Father James Porter. He was supposed to be sodomizing little boys, although small girls were all right with him, too. He is in prison for a long time, charged with molesting at least a hundred helpless young in the Fall River area alone. He never could have left so many shaken young without the bishops and Cardinal Bernard Law, of Boston, who transferred him from the last wounded parish to the next unsuspecting one, and who don't even visit him in prison.

Williamson said she still had sexually transmitted diseases. She appeared to struggle to hold herself together against unannounced assaults of her memory. The hardest thing about being mugged by memory was the first thought that she was guilty of whatever it was that erupted in her.

For our second meeting, I didn't have to do more than walk three blocks from my house to where Diana Williamson lives in a building looking out on the Hudson River. She is forty-six. Williamson is a thin woman with her hair in locks that are covered with colored beads. She said that her memory first turned against her when she came out of a dental office at 57th Street and Sixth Avenue in Manhattan and walked out to a cab that was stopped at a light. She was going to her job as an oncology fellow at the New York University Medical Center at First Avenue and 30th Street. Because of the anesthesia, she didn't hear the cabdriver claiming that he had an appointment at the airport. She got in the cab and sat motionless. He told her again he was going to the airport. Still, she didn't move. Now the driver got out of the front and, swearing at this black bitch, opened the rear door, grabbed her arm, and yanked her out of the cab. Her shoulder was wrenched. There was a bang as her head hit the cab roof. Diana came out of the cab wincing in pain and squalling for a cop. The cabdriver, Marius Agagiu, was convicted of third degree assault after a bench trial before Judge Leona Friedman on October 4, 1988.

She kept remembering the sound of her head hitting the cab. She was at New York University Medical Center in the second floor laboratory, where she worked on an Elisa test that would prove HIV. She split her night hours and days off between extra duty at St. Clare's Hospital, which handled mostly AIDS, and the Bellevue emergency room, which is the Yankee Stadium of trauma.

At the end of one day, she took off her lab coat and went out to First Avenue. Going from the hospital entrance she went by a river of people in pain, so many physical, but simultaneously, an inordinate number of mentally disturbed. She walked down to her apartment on 23rd Street. She put on a Marvin Gaye album and a tape of a Seinfeld show on HBO. She took her full bottle of Valium, Elavil, Xanax, and other pills that she had hoarded. When Marvin Gaye got to her song, "What's Going On?" she swallowed the entire bottle. She remembers staying on the bed and listening to the music and Seinfeld.

A friend found her almost dead the next morning and took her back to Bellevue. She told the residents in the emergency room that it was not a suicide attempt. She made a mistake, that's all. How could she have done anything else? Didn't she work right here?

She doesn't know how long it was after that, but she was living with a friend in an apartment at 1265 Park Avenue, and she remembers a dark fear draping itself all over her. She was alone in the apartment. She didn't even put on Marvin Gaye. When they carried her out to an ambulance in the morning, it was the start of consistent torment, the origins of which she did not know. She remembers two things: the sound of a head banging and something to do with braids. Not hers, but somebody's.

She took a studio apartment on 51st Street for six hundred dollars. Halfway through the night, she remembers waking up, staring hard at the darkness, then reaching for her full bottle of pills. Of course it was full. Between hospital pharmacies and her own prescription blanks, she was able to hoard enough to kill herself. She woke up in St. Clare's Hospital. She had no idea how she got there. As it was an obvious suicide attempt, the doctors at St. Clare's wanted to hold her. She talked them out of it by identifying herself as a coworker. The overdose was unintentional, she said. She walked out of the hospital, saw a for rent sign on a building and took a ground floor garden apartment for a thousand dollars a month. She doesn't know which apartment she then was in, but she knows that she woke up once after swallowing another bottle of pills and was in a locked room in Roosevelt Hospital. She didn't know whether she called 911 or if the super in the building took her there.

She does know that she had the third apartment, on West 23rd, that cost her another eight hundred dollars a month. Whether she had all three or two at once is unknown to her. She knows the drugs she took. This time, she took a flock of tricyclic antidepressant pills, Q-T interval, and that did it. She survived. Through a daze, she decided that pills wouldn't do it. The next time, a knife. Her record of trying suicide almost by the hour, however, brought in the courts. Diana heard three pens scratching names on official papers. She was committed involuntarily to Columbia Presbyterian's psychiatric center. They held her for thirteen months. The head banging still was heard, but this time it didn't cause her to lose control of herself. Banging and braids.

Even when she was released, her mind was going down hallways that took her nowhere. Then in 1992, she was found wandering in the middle of the night, and a cop called an ambulance and she was back in a hospital. This time, they brought in a psychiatrist, Dr. Paula Eagle, who began long sessions with her.

At one of them, I met Eagle informally and talked with Williamson for a while. Then I said good-bye and left and got outside and now my own mother was sitting upstairs on her bed with a pistol and pulling the trigger. The clicks were so loud in my head that I could hear nothing else. I was probably nine. I looked in. The one scene of her sitting on the bed with the pistol stunned me. I said something about giving me the gun and her answer was to scream, "Get out of here!" with such force that I ran downstairs and told my grandmother. I held my finger to my temple like a gun. She went upstairs and took the pistol from my mother and came back downstairs confused and angered. Upstairs, my mother shrieked. I was afraid to go near her.

I don't know how long it took me to get over that. I'll let you know.

I remembered my mother in a scene here, a vision there, over the next few months. I did not know how much of her she was going to show me.

The bottom of Williamson's mind came rising in small pieces, rising, rising, rising, and always bringing her closer to the banging and braids. "I went to college at St. John's with Diana," Jared Mc-Callister was saying. He now is a reporter and columnist on the New York *Daily News.* "Something always was bothering her. Nobody knew what it was. Then these stories started coming out of Boston, and she started talking about what had happened to her. That seemed to be the way it happened around the country. There would be a story in the papers, and then people who had been abused would come forward."

Now, she drains cans of Coke as she goes back over her life.

For her first six years she was in poor Brooklyn, on Eastern Parkway, a wide street with trees and a heritage of the best white working class any city ever has seen. When people of color moved in—Diana's family was Cuban and large—it became a street of struggles. The whites fled. Diana and her two sisters lived there with their parents. The father was usually drunk or drugged. One day he passed out on the living room couch. The mother had her family come over and carry out furniture. The father did not move. The mother packed bags and took the girls with her to their grandmother's house. They never saw the father again. The grandmother lived on a crowded and desolate street called Park Place, a brawling street of drugs and guns. Diana lived on the ground floor. All she had to do was hold an arm out the window to be in the middle of a gunfight. One morning she came out of the house to find a dead man in the gutter.

One side of the Williamson family was a Cuban scrimmage of guns and quarrels and shrieking at cops to arrest one of them. One brother was dead from something. Diana's mother, who was assaulted by an uncle in Cuba, had a son at fourteen. She then remarried and had three girls, Diana being the second oldest. A cousin, Louis Taylor, shot his girlfriend. His brother, Ronnie, went to a witness in the hospital and threatened to kill her. Louis is still in Otisville, New York, this time on drug charges. Ronnie is in a prison whose name people aren't sure of, although Diana thinks it is Sing Sing. Diana remembers the visiting room at some prison where the children were given coins to get the worst food out of the vending machines so they wouldn't bother the woman and prisoner during their visit. Diana needed only dimes, ten percent of what a kid needs in a visiting room today.

At home, there were boxes of drug money in closets and the grandmother practicing Santeria, the Cuban voodoo form of Catholicism, with Saint Barbara on one side of a holy medal and the great Chango, the god of fire and violence, on the opposite side. The grandmother slashed the neck of a live chicken and poured the blood out for her ceremonies and then cooked the chicken for dinner. Seeing the blood before dinner, Diana never wanted to eat.

She does not know the first time she was abused. It was at night, and by one of her cousins, she said. He put his hand into her pajamas and rubbed her. She remembers squirming and crying. It was to happen again.

Diana's mother worked in a factory in Brooklyn and sold bras and panties on the streets of Bedford-Stuyvesant. She also worked in a dry cleaner and candy store Diana's grandmother owned downstairs from their apartment at 1575 Park Place. The grandmother also owned a bodega around the corner that was held up several times.

The mother had three sisters, and they all competed with each other to put their children in the best schools. They stretched their money to the limit to pay tuitions. After that, they tiptoed up to the closet shelf, reached up and took bursar money out of the shoe boxes of receipts from drug peddling.

One side of the family also went the other way. Diana's uncle,

Rene Cubas, Sr., was a reporter for the Spanish language paper *Tiempo,* and he then went to work for Madison Square Garden's boxing press department. I knew him from the 1971 fight between Muhammad Ali and Joe Frazier, which drew a spectacular sports crowd. I sat with Bernadette Devlin of Northern Ireland. Cubas came around to say hello. I never knew a thing about his family and couldn't imagine that I ever would.

Cubas's son, Rene, Jr., is Diana Williamson's nephew. His mother, Diana's aunt, had a beauty parlor on 168th Street and Hillside Avenue in the Jamaica section of Queens. On the way to the bus terminal down the block for the ride home, Rene, Jr., would stop at the beauty shop. He remembers hearing his mother and some of the other women talking about Diana having trouble. "You've got to remember that they were Cuban and very secretive," Rene was saying one afternoon. "But over time I heard them saying she wasn't well because of the school, that something happened at the school. After listening to them a lot, I thought that something evil had attacked Diana. It was sex. I thought they were talking about lesbians attacking her. What did I know? I was a kid. I never thought of a priest."

Catholic word of mouth told Diana's mother about Sacred Heart, which was Catholic and in Fair Haven, Massachusetts, across the bridge from New Bedford, far away from Park Place, where at the height of the drug crack there were shootings by the hour. So many mothers left themselves nearly penniless in order to get their children to a school where there was no gunfire. Sacred Heart school took children from first grade on, and if they would do this, if the school would raise and educate a child in a religious atmosphere and away from the violence at Park Place, it must be a fine school. She and another little girl, Andrea Randall, were of color in a school of 150 whites.

The first time I went to look at Sacred Heart school, I went to the wrong place, a strange place, a church that was named the Convent Church of Sacred Hearts of Jesus and Mary. A nun in a pale blue habit answered the convent door. She said she was from the Philippines and she and a half dozen others were brought here by the Bishop of Fall River to reopen this church, which had closed in 1993. The nuns pray from 5:30 A.M. until deep in the night in a tiny chapel and a larger church. They have no other real life. The nun walked silently through the chapel and into the church and, after that, directed me to the Sacred Heart Academy, which was a few blocks down the road. She said good-bye sweetly and closed the door to her unfathomable life.

Down the street was the old Sacred Heart Academy dormitory. The building is there but the school is gone. An elderly woman told me that the school was now a residence for seniors. The last person associated with the old boarding school, a priest named Sullivan, had just been buried.

Behind the school there was a cement staircase of two hundred steps. When she displeased the nuns, Diana says, they made her kneel and pray on each step as she went up to her bed. In her first year there, at age six, a priest, James R. Porter, took her to the basement and forced anal sex on her. Diana remembers pain and fighting but she was held down. "I always was held down."

Drinking one of her Cokes, she recalled some of her times at Sacred Heart. The priest she recalls is Porter, who took Diana and a couple of others, boys included, to the basement of a church either in New Bedford or Fall River, where they abused, raped, and sodomized the children.

There were weekend nights when Porter or one of the priests with him, came into the school and told Diana and a few others to come along and they would get ice cream. There was a stand a short distance away that sold soft ice cream.

"The only nun who was of color was a novice," Diana was saying. "She went along to help manage us. She told us to be quiet and do what the priests tell you.

"Porter drove us over the bridge to a church in New Bedford, where we were taken to the basement and Porter drank and gave us whisky and had us undress. Porter took pictures of us. We were standing there naked. The flashbulbs frightened me when they went off. Then he took us into back rooms that had easy chairs or small couches . . . and molested us.

"When they brought us back to school," Diana Williamson was saying, "the nun working as school nurse always did for us. Sew up the rips. This went on every year I was in that school." She explained that Porter "liked children because an older girl said no. We never refused. We were afraid even to move. I kept it hidden from my family and myself."

In the car taking them to another church basement one night, Andrea Randall, one of the seven-year-olds, began to cry. The nun in the front told her to stop. This she would not do. Diana recalls, "The nun told Andrea Randall that it would be easier if she shut up. Andrea was crying and wouldn't stop. So the nun leaned over the seat. She leaned over the seat and hit Andrea hard. Then she grabbed Andrea's hair and hit her head against that post there in the back of the station wagon. Slammed it. When we got to the church where they had their party, Andrea couldn't get out of the car. She stayed there while we were taken inside. Andrea was not in classes the next day. There was a large bump on her right forehead. Her speech was slurred. I remember Andrea dragging her leg as she walked. In class, Andrea began crying. She said she couldn't see. The nun took her from class. Then at night they came in and carried her out of the sleeping room. It was the last time we saw Andrea. One night, one of the teachers, this older man who used a cane, told us, 'Andrea is an angel.' "

Diana remembered and told Dr. Eagle that she stayed in bed a lot on Mondays because of the rough sex on her little body over the weekend. Diana Williamson's life remains badly dented: with a sexually transmitted disease whose silent symptoms did not show until she was twenty-one.

James R. Porter is currently in Bridgewater Detention Center for the Sexually Dangerous. He is there for assaulting over a hundred children around the lower part of Massachusetts. One, Tom Fulchino from St. Julia's in Weston, another town, was twelve, he told the *Boston Globe* investigative team, when he was slowest to leave his grammar school building after an evening activity in 1960, and Father James Porter "got me then and just, just got me down on the ground and was going like a madman . . . just . . . I understand this: He was humping me like a dog."

Cardinal Law of Boston said Porter's crimes had nothing to do with him. He said it was the fault of one person, James R. Porter. He said that only these anti-Catholic news reporters made it important. Law announced his solution:

"By all means we call down God's power on the media, particularly *The Boston Globe.*"

Over her Coke, Diana Williamson challenged me to answer why Porter had not been given a longer prison sentence.

People would find it more outrageous if Porter was caught this time sodomizing a young boy. They seem unaware that women have been hideously abused in the church perhaps as often as males.

Diana Williamson went on to Catholic high school in Brooklyn and college, St. John's, and then to Mt. Sinai Medical School in Manhattan. She specializes in HIV and AIDS patients. So many of them are homeless and virtually all are dead broke. She now is the director of Crossroads Medical Center in Brooklyn.

Chapter Eight

L et me take you to the other side of the street, to an old revered Brooklyn neighborhood, Bushwick, and tell you about John Powis, whose hooded eyes mask a gleam of love for absolutely everything at hand. Just by his presence, he stands for those priests who work religiously for the poor and anguished, but unlike Powis, were more silent than the statues in the presence of evil in their own halls. John Powis, who has been through it all, pushes for his own idea of what must be right. I don't know one person, and after all these years in news I know many, who at the start of this book didn't tell me that I could not do this without writing about John Powis.

He was in the last months of his career as a parish priest when I walked into his church for the first time. He had Parkinson's, and cancer on one foot and he was exhausted and depressed by the ceaseless pain of so many of his people. Then he would be aroused by the extraordinary dumb acts of his diocese. And he would be elated by the celebrations of life by any parishioners. He didn't have long to go, but he wasn't going to drop dead of boredom.

At his church, St. Barbara's, on this afternoon, during a rehearsal for a wedding, the bride, a young and beautiful Latina, yet essentially made of steel cord, is pushing the groom around like he was a coatrack, and why shouldn't she, the world knows that the woman is strong and the man is nothing but a dog in a tuxedo.

"Put them down!" the bride said.

"I'm just looking," the groom said.

The bride had her new shoes on a ledge in the church vestibule and the groom had the nerve to have them out of the box.

"Leave them alone and get where you belong," she said.

"Where?"

"Right here with your brother."

She indicated a spot a couple of paces away.

"Is this how you want it?" John Powis said.

"Yes, Father."

"Then he'll be right here," Powis said. He touched the groom's arm and eased into his spot in front of a doorway that opened right onto an aisle that ran down the side of the church and up to the altar.

"When I say to you, you walk straight up to the altar and wait for me to come," the bride said to the groom. He nodded.

"Whatever you wish," Powis said to her. "It's your day."

The bridesmaids now had the wedding shoes out of the box again and were noisily examining them. People passing by on the street looked up the church steps and at the bridesmaids in the open doorway.

"You go with your brother when you hear the organ," the bride told the groom.

"You ought to come to the wedding," Powis said to me. "It'll be a wonderful wedding. These are lovely people."

The excitement was marvelous, the humor contagious and, simultaneously, it was anguishing to see that much of this brightness should be everywhere else, but has been suffocated by suspicion and denial.

On that first Sunday when I came from "the city," as people who live in Brooklyn call Manhattan, I audited the twelve-thirty mass that John Powis was saying at St. Barbara's on Central Avenue in Bushwick. The high towers, built when people believed in building pyramids to Christ, rise out of streets where people have virtually nothing. The church can hold one thousand and more who pray in the pale light coming from stained glass high up in a ceiling that speaks of the Mediterranean. Powis stands on this altar as the best symbol of his church of the past. The Brooklyn diocese says there are 187 priests for 217 parishes. The priests are at least aging. Powis is sixty-nine. In the nation, only one-third of the Catholic parishes, once the battleships of the religion, have priests. Around the world, one parish in six has a priest. In the seminaries around New York, there are perhaps a half dozen hopeful priests in training. I was at the funeral mass for my friend, Monsignor Jack Barry, when, in one of his last acts, Cardinal John O'Connor of New York arose and said that there were only seven seminarians at the Dunwoodie Seminary and that if anybody wanted to become a priest, he, O'Connor, would personally drive them right now to the campus. Soon, people will be stepping out of congregations everywhere and running the place or there will be no place. Your next priests must be elected by the parishioners, like St. Augustine. Now, the religion withers and the sexual crimes enrage. The dismissal of them as merely unfortunate transgressions, and the cover-up and obstruction by people running the church causes underground fires that maybe never can be extinguished.

One idea that has been advanced is for the Catholics to have a huge consecration of hosts by priests and then have them distributed to parishes who have no priests but do have the deacons, or whatever, who can distribute them. This is taken from the Jewish practice of rabbis officiating and declaring food kosher. It then goes out into the markets.

John Powis must do his own work, which is to find the glee in people and bring it out for all to see. He sees a smile as an expression given to us by Christ, although the fishermen who left stories of him never once said we had a Lord who smiled or made you laugh.

At mass, a mother was in the pew in front of me with her little girl, who was dressed in white for her birthday. Part of the celebration was for her to stand at the front of the church while everybody sang "Happy Birthday." They do this for all birthdays at St. Barbara's and the little girl kept asking her mother, "Now?" and the mother shook her head and gave the answer of every parent: "Soon."

Suddenly, and I didn't know how it happened and neither did the mother in front of me, but all the other people with birthdays were up at the altar and John Powis was leading the church in a loud "Happy Birthday" and she and her daughter were not there.

The best the little girl could do was get in the aisle and cry. The mother was crestfallen. She picked up her daughter and started up the aisle, but Powis had finished the song.

The four or five hundred at the mass sat. Powis was about to resume his prayers when he saw the mother and the girl in white.

Powis said to the girl, "Didn't they sing 'Happy Birthday' for you?"

She shook her head no.

The mother called out, "She was not there for this."

"Well," Powis said, "we're going to sing 'Happy Birthday' for her."

The church stood. The choir, off to Powis's left, stood. He raised a hand to lead everybody in "Happy Birthday." This song was the one and only one written by the Hill sisters in Kentucky about a thousand years ago. It belongs to the publisher and their foundation. The Hill sisters led sleepless lives for years because of the big lumps of money in the mattresses. The song still brings in two million a year.

Now in St. Barbara's, they sang the encore loudly, everybody did, and the mother stood alone in front of the church holding her little girl in white and the mother was openly thrilled and the little girl listened intently. At the end, the church exploded into applause.

Chapter Nine

John Powis smiles at today and smiles at tomorrow, for the air he breathes is made of hope. He is known by generations of Latinos who often survive only on his ability to catch people who start wandering in despair and bring them back to try again and hope with him. He is one of the invisible people of his city without whom there would be only a city in pieces.

He works himself sick in a parish of people who crowd into his rectory after a fire: "The woman was burned out of her apartment last night," he says, indicating a beleaguered woman in the hallway. "With five children. She had no place to go. The Red Cross took them in. I don't know where they go now." One of his people is Luis Garden Acosta, who went from the streets to Harvard and came back to found a famous city school, El Puente, that teaches Latinos how to overcome disease of race by schooling. But he is only one person and there are so many others affected by John Powis.

Then there was the night with twenty-two hundred in the auditorium at Boys and Girls High School in Bedford-Stuyvesant, in Brooklyn. Since this was an endeavor of the poor, nobody came to write about it, or put it on television. They were mostly from the East Brooklyn churches, which are the story of the city in our time. They are descendants of Saul Alinsky, who put Chicago toughness into civic work: Selfish interests come first. Don't dare try to move half your welfare roll next door to people who have small houses and backyards, and that is all they have and ever will have. You spread the welfare people out as if they are just like you, into a lot of neighborhoods and if people don't want it, you help them get used to it.

The East Brooklyn churches became a civic group when the drug crack was a zephyr streaking through the streets of small chances. Powis served 450 funerals in 1994 and '95, with AIDS and gunfire the primary causes. Ministers of any faith demanded that police protect Latin and black neighborhoods as if they were filled with decent whites. It was the first time in the history of the city's famous police department that the poor of color received white protection. The ministers risked their lives by turning in drug and gun spots to police. John Powis was giving names and addresses; it was the true work of the Lord. The violence faded and fear fell. The mayor, Giuliani, took an extraordinary number of curtain calls for what he had decided was his vision.

The East Brooklyn churches also built the first housing in burned out parts of Brooklyn. In honor of this at the meeting, they had on a wide screen over the stage their tabernacle: a large color projection of a new house, the white gleaming, the bricks bright. They applauded a mention of the Williamsburg Bridge. When ministers got up and called out their areas, places only this crowd knows these days—"Mott Haven!"—the people roared. They spent the night demanding housing, just as they had for police protection. One of their leaders in the auditorium was John Powis, who sat with a group from his church.

"This is the way church should be," he said. It is, where he comes from.

They raised Powis on the theology of the worst of the west of Ireland. The countries of rocky land and cold rain exported a religion so constricted it was a wonder people could take a deep breath.

The old St. Sylvester's Parish, which might as well have been in county Mayo, is on the border between Brooklyn and Queens. Because of this, the neighborhood is called City Line. He is from a family of ten of a Welsh father and Italian mother. His father worked for the National City Bank and never did earn over $5,000 a year. In the Depression, the family moved so many times that John Powis can't recall them, although he knows that once they sold their house for fifty dollars and bought another down the block for about the same amount.

He grew up when St. Sylvester's had a pastor, James Smith, who patrolled under the el on Fulton Street with a bullwhip whose crack was louder than the traffic or the el overhead. Let one kid try to sneak into the Earl movie house for films listed as "condemned" or "objectionable in part" in the Brooklyn Catholic paper, *The Tablet,* that got the list from the national Legion of Decency. Of course the bad movies were the only movies that kids wanted to see.

If there were any women from the parish in the saloon on the corner of Grant and Glenmore enjoying a day-off drink, and there sure were women in there, Priest Smith walked in and held up the whip for all to see and chased the women.

When women arrived for weddings dressed not quite to the breasts, Smith was at the church doors with large white Turkish towels over his arm. All women he judged as indecent had to wrap a towel around their shoulders.

From the start, John Powis was going to become a priest. Father Smith had a huge effect on him that consisted of Powis going to the other side of the street the first chance he got. All he ever wanted when he was coming up was a church for worship, parishioners he could help, and a baseball field where he could watch games. After he got his first job, at a major-league baseball park, and at the same time was a seminarian studying to become a priest of his church, a glorious ambition, he creaked with the uneasiness of feeling that he had been given too much.

The beer cooling system has given out at the famous marble *rotunder* at the ballpark once known as Ebbets Field, where he had his first job. He was working the concession stand in this large ballpark lobby, whose name came from the marble floor and led to all the lower tier gates. The Dodgers played here. It is in the middle of the second game of a doubleheader that starts at 2:05 P.M. and has a long, long way to go. An inning or so back, John Powis, pulling that tap beer, found no icy feel to the twelve-ounce container. Powis was immediately thankful that the sign on his concession stand said, BEER and not COLD BEER, for then he wouldn't be able to sell any. He was honest to the sip.

There were several gates off the rotunda leading to the best lower-deck seats. On the field, a pitcher was being changed, and therefore charging through the gates and slapping into the counter with hands out came the Brooklyn beer drinkers.

"What?"

"Is?"

"This?"

Holding beer that tasted as if it just came out in the sun, here were legitimate Brooklyn baseball fans, who wanted beer and wanted it in time to race back up the steps and catch the first pitch of the relief pitcher. And John Powis, counterman, Harry M. Stevens caterer, had just handed them hot beer.

"What is this?"

"What?" John Powis said.

"It isn't cold. Give me another."

"It's all the same," Powis said.

"You can't do no better?"

"I'm sorry. I don't make the beer," he told them.

"Do something."

Powis had heard of one thing to do at a time like this, and he couldn't do it: get cold water someplace and turn it into cold beer.

By the late innings of the second game, doubleheaders were wearing and often embarrassing for John Powis and his friend Neil Sullivan. They got the job when a man named Kelly in the office of caterer Harry M. Stevens looked at their job applications and saw they were studying to be Catholic priests.

"Please work for us," Kelly said. "They're robbing us here."

Kelly had such faith in his church that he assigned Powis and Sullivan to work the best counter. Powis remembers being given stacks of wax containers with the green HARRY M. STEVENS around the top.

The containers were counted back in the Stevens office. The beer cost thirty-five cents. At the end of the day, the receipts had to equal the number of containers that a counterman had used. Similarly, the hot dogs were counted and the receipts, at thirty-five cents each, had to match the numbers missing and presumed sold.

The doubleheaders were grotesque for each product.

The beer was warm.

The hot dogs, cooked in water, changed color as the game went on. They were pink and then red and by the seventh inning of the second game they were green. When people were appalled at the color, Powis told them, "Put plenty of mustard on and you won't notice a thing."

And he could not believe his fortune. He was going to be a priest and that is all he ever wanted. Minister to people. On any Friday night when the Dodgers were out of town, he went to the Catholic Worker center on East 1st Street in Manhattan. This was where Dorothy Day conducted meetings about serving God by helping the poor about you. She was everybody's saint. The notion, in later years, that you could place such approval and faith in a Mother Teresa, shows how susceptible, how vulnerable, how defenseless religious people are in the modern life. Dorothy Day of the fifties served food to the poor in sandals. Mother Teresa of the nineties called politicians for helicopters.

That was in the forties and fifties. Life then grew even harsher. Blacks came on buses from the South, these sad-faced women with arms leaden from holding babies on the long ride from Montgomery, Alabama, Orangeburg, South Carolina, Durham, North Carolina, and the Tidewater area of Virginia. They had been driven off the cotton fields by the John Deere 1099 cotton picker. At the same time, tremendous economic deprivation in Puerto Rico had late-night flights from San Juan packed with people going to mix, often nastily, with the blacks.

As a parish priest, Powis was in the Brooklyn neighborhoods of Brownsville and Bushwick and Bedford-Stuyvesant. He could go weeks and the only whites he would see would be the cops, garbage collectors, and the odd deliveryman. The people were living close to the bone then, and are still today. Even more so. After so many elections that were supposed to change the world for all, and mostly those on the bottom, people poor and of color have gone from living in faded buildings to being forced out of them, as painters paraded in to make the place neat for the young whites to take over. The fortunate with jobs packed the A train and Livonia Avenue el to ride like horses being transported to reach jobs in Manhattan. A lot were jobless because they had no jobs. Half the blacks at least are jobless. Brownsville was famous for one company that ran its business from the back of a candy store on Saratoga Avenue. The candy store was Midnight Rose's and the company was Murder, Inc. The elite went into show business, most prominent being Danny Kaye, who has a junior high school named for him that is a few blocks from the high school he attended, Thomas Jefferson.

Two books had been written about just one street in Brownsville, Amboy Street—*The Amboy Dukes,* a wonderful love novel by

Irving Shulman, and *Murder, Inc.,* by Sid Feder of the Associated Press, which is just what it sounds like. A few of the other streets are chronicled in the Sing Sing death house logs.

When Powis was pastor of Our Lady of Presentation church in Bedford-Stuyvesant, the air had the smell and sound of gunfire. When a collection basket was passed at Presentation, the people in the pews searched their pockets for change. The only way to pay the bills was with proceeds from Wednesday night bingo games at the Eastern Parkway Arena, which was once a fight club.

One Thursday night, Powis sat in his office in the church with the previous night's bingo receipts in a safe in the closet behind him. He listened to the troubles of parishioners, who waited in an outer office until Powis could see them. Here was a woman with a son in trouble, another woman whose husband was untrustworthy, at least, a couple being evicted, an arrangement for a baptism, and then the last of this night, two women and a man who had been waiting for an hour and a half. One of the women said that her brother was up for parole but had to list someone who would counsel him when he got out. "Could he come by here and see you sometimes?" she asked.

"Of course," Powis said. "Let's do that right now." Powis took out a sheet of church stationery. He remembers saying, "State parole," as he started writing. Powis felt something. He looked up. There were three .45s pointed at his head.

"Give it up," the woman said. She was thin and had dead eyes.

He stared at the dial of the safe. He couldn't think of the numbers. He started to turn the dial with no idea of what he was doing.

"I can't remember the combination," Powis said. He was new in the parish and the last pastor had given him the safe combination, but he had misplaced it and right now couldn't remember it.

"We usually blow the head off some white man take his time," the woman said.

Suddenly, the hand of God joined Powis's on the dial. He had no idea of what he was doing, but he twirled and the safe clicked open.

"You almost dead," the woman said.

They took $1,800 in bingo money—one thousand for the next night's bank and eight hundred profit, handcuffed Powis, taped his mouth and locked him in the closet.

After a lot of kicking, the other priest in the rectory at the time came in and got him out.

Later, the detective from the 79th Precinct asked Powis, "Do you know any of them?" He had photos spread on Powis's desk.

The woman's dead brown eyes stared from one picture. "I know her," Powis said, pointing to the picture.

"You're sure," the detective said.

"Oh, yes, I know her. She said she'd blow my head off."

"Father, I think that you're the first white man she didn't blow the head off. She's Joanne Chesimard."

And just before coming in on Powis, Chesimard and the two with her had blown the head completely off of a landlord at Sutter and Howard Avenues, a few blocks away from Powis's church. Chesimard also had killed a state trooper on the New Jersey turnpike.

Fran and Wayne Barrett, who loved Powis and who lived a couple of blocks away, and were frightened out of their breaths, piled into the rectory.

"I'm wonderful," Powis told them. "A great thing happened. She didn't kill me."

They caught Chesimard and put her in Clinton, New Jersey prison for life plus sixty-five years. Then three visitors pulled .45s and took her out of the prison and she fled to Cuba in 1979, where she remains.

Powis had persuaded his diocese to let him spend a couple of years studying Spanish in Puerto Rico under Ivan Illich, a priest out of New York who was a favorite of Cardinal Spellman's because of his language abilities. Powis was there in 1960 and 1962. Illich was such a success as a teacher of the language and the culture that the bishops, paying their curates' way to learn languages, had no idea of how much he despised the rich. He was constantly fighting the Catholic church in Puerto Rico, which consisted of elegant dining and swimming pools in the gardens behind the houses. Powis learned Spanish and was excited by Illich's ideas that hospitals and schools had to be changed.

The first time I ever heard of John Powis was in 1968 when forty thousand schoolteachers' union members, as angry as boars, marched around City Hall and shouted curses from the bottom of the earth. The teachers were marching against decentralization and community control of schools. These terms meant neighborhood blacks firing white teachers whom they believed were producing poor results. Which they were. Worse than that. They threw up their hands and said that we can't stop illiteracy. Pay us anyway. Powis was a priest who was elected to the school board of the Ocean Hill-Brownsville district. His doctrine was directly from Ivan Illich. Schools had to be changed so people of color could learn.

As an Ocean Hill-Brownsville school board officer, he fired a white teacher, Fred Nauman, a union chapter chairman. The people of color in the neighborhood thought Nauman and the rest of the white union was racist. As did Powis. He acted. The union reacted. They put enough people into the streets to defend the Atlantic shoreline.

The teachers picketed during the day. The city's white labor leaders, nearly all Catholic, were at the bar at night in the old Toots Shor's in Manhattan, To them, the strike was personal, and far beyond schoolteachers. The great white unions, the electrical workers and heavy equipment and bricklayers and carpenters, wanted to keep blacks out forever. Gerry Ryan of the fire union put the strike in a sentence: "They want a piece of the pie and they're not going to get it."

The teachers union was to win and white writers called it "The Strike That Changed New York and America."

One book writer said that "Powis' political philosophy was closer to anarchism than anything else."

This was far too orderly for Powis.

He then became the head of the Ocean Hill-Brownsville Tenants Association. They took over twenty-three decaying apartment buildings supposedly being run by the city. He collected rents, to pay the city, keeping people from eviction, and paid for whatever repairs that could be afforded. He next was with a project called Grace Towers, where 168 people were thrown out. He brought them all down to his rectory. The fire department sent men around to chase them out. Powis had his people stay where they were. Cots were donated and the people slept in hallways and offices. The fire department finally stationed a man in the second floor hallway, with a hook and extinguisher all night. The people and the fireman stayed for eight weeks. Food was sent from churches all over Brooklyn. It was how he lived his life.

At all times in these neighborhoods, Powis worked in the lion's mouth. People had started to believe that they must fight for their rights. A housing activist named Curly Erstermera ran a group called God's War Against People Oppression. Police raided his apartment at 354 Saratoga Avenue and found a room full of bazookas, and the wall scrawled with Mao's pronouncements on the difference between a bandit and a revolutionary.

"You're going to have to stop being around these people," a police inspector said to Powis.

"I can't," Powis said. "They are very good tenant organizers."

Chapter Ten

No anger can seem more just than the reaction to the sex scandals in places most unexpected, where you always have walked. Leaving John Powis's church, it is only blocks to St. Pancras in Glendale, where I got married, and where nothing ever should happen, and now I have dreary business. And from there, it is straight up only a few more blocks to St. Matthias in Ridgewood, where, again, nothing ever should have gone wrong, and now Helen Wolf waits to see me on this Sunday to express searing anger at a priest.

Helen Wolf's voice was afire as she called me to report sex molestations by a priest, Father Brian Keller, in St. Matthias parish. I made a date to meet her after she finished her Sunday mass duties. She sang the mass. I was in the Glendale Diner, only a few blocks away from St. Matthias. Danny Collins was with me for coffee. I mentioned that many people were calling me with complaints against priests and bishops, leaving me dazed.

At one time, the only discordant sound to happen in Glendale was a mailman delivering late payment notices. I didn't think that things could be any different now. I mentioned that Helen and her friends wanted to sink a priest named Brian Keller.

"Keller? Big red-headed guy?"

"I don't know what he looks like. His name is Brian Keller."

"That's sounds familiar. I'm trying to remember whether he was in St. Margaret's or St. Pancras. I think it was at St. Pancras. I remember somebody saying they wouldn't let their little girl alone in the room with him. I think I heard that. I didn't keep track of priests. They're like baseball players, the way they get traded one place to another. I'll ask Glenn, see what he thinks."

Glenn is Glenn Prine, who is from the neighborhood, and it turned out that he was unsure about Keller. You know the parish you're in all right, but a priest, especially one that is in and out of the place, gets lost in your memory. Because of this, at least some molesters get away.

I went from the diner up several blocks to see Helen Wolf at St. Matthias. The church name was so much in the blood that, when asked where they were from, people answered: "St. Benny's." That was my St. Benedict Joseph.

Or, "St. Pascal Baylon."

"Where do you work?"

"Liberty Avenue. St. Elizabeth's." Every woman saint was considered a virgin by Rome or she would not have been named. But nobody knows who they are and we are deprived forever of knowing about such extraordinarily lofty virtue.

The churches had basketball teams in their halls and basements. The games were reported in the first paper I worked for, the *Long Island Daily Press*. In the sports department we spent many hours writing headlines saying, "St. John's Batters St. Teresa's, 45–38."

St. Matthias always was a German-Catholic neighborhood of attached stone houses whose stoops glisten from so much scrubbing that meals can be served on them. Polished windows are blinding in the sunlight. They wash with vinegar and wipe with paper. In the morning, you saw the children scrubbing the family bar, Kiyoodles, before going to school.

The people always conformed and obeyed. The most revered

and powerful person was the priest. Police captains removed their hats in his presence. Suddenly, shockingly, Helen Wolf, who lived every hour of her life inside a walled faith, calls a newspaper for purposes of an attempted ruining of a priest's career.

At church, Helen Wolf was up on the altar, singing gloriously, singing in long, beautiful notes that washed delightfully over the rows of pews and rose to a dome ceiling that was covered with paintings. Flames of light came through a circle of stained glass windows. She saw me as I came in. Helen Wolf was on the left side of the altar and under the music she was seething and wanted to come down off the altar and tell me whatever she recalled or heard about a priest named Brian Keller.

She told me that she and two of her friends had been molested by him. The brother of one of them, Bobby Schmidt, now a father of two, who had kept his memory of being molested hidden in turmoil in the pit of his stomach for years, sat in a pew and made up his mind to talk to me.

The row I was in had a brass plaque saying the pew was in memory of Siegfried H. Jakob. The one behind me was for Jacob Graf.

Helen Wolf's parents were Gottscheers, from the border of Yugoslavia and Austria. Her father was a cabinetmaker. The Wolfs followed all laws, with one above all: the priest is right. It took Helen years to collect enough anger to confront a priest. Helen Wolf was not doing it as part of a lawsuit. She was doing it because she wanted to hurt and ruin the priest and everybody who did nothing about this priest who had molested her and her friends of both sexes.

Even now, one generation, maybe two away from the habits of the old country, only a few would dare raise their voice against the rule of the church.

Once, people were such blind followers that they even obeyed breweries, which were the commercial center of the area. Joseph

Eppig's brewery on Grove and Linden, only a few streets away from the church, sold beer in bottles that were labeled in raised glass, "This Bottle MUST Be Returned When Empty."

Now Helen Wolf had her right hand waving in the air as she led the four hundred—counted by ushers—in the singing of the Lord's Prayer. Then down the aisle came the recessional. First, there was a young girl in a white robe holding a staff and cross, her oval face so serious. Behind her was the priest, very old and the sparse hair white. Following him, holding books, singing, were six women, parishioners. At which point I wanted to see them all drop through the floor. I could hear some priest, bishop or whatever, insulting you by cooing, "Why, we honor our women. We allow them to come to the altar and escort the priest at mass's end. They take part in our ceremonies."

And I could hear all the women nodding and smiling so sweetly. "Yes, Father, that's right, Father."

Afterwards, Helen stood under the large choir loft, and said that was where Keller started.

"We were twelve and thirteen. Oh, he was right with us. He had reddish hair and played the organ with energy. If you came early and left late and smiled at him, he took you to his summer house in Manahawkin, New Jersey. People thought it was fine. The kids were going with the priest!

"The parents let the kids go?"

"The kids were going with the priest! My mother had an aneurysm burst when she was nine and had severe memory trouble. But she didn't forget that a priest was the most important person to her family. My father was uncomfortable. Keller came into the kitchen too cheerfully. But my father couldn't say this to his wife. So he said nothing.

"We all went to Jersey and jumped off the pier into the water. Keller swam up to Bobby Schmidt, who was twelve, and pulled his trunks down and put his hand onto the genitals. Then he came onto Schmidt's sister, Heidi, and put his hand down her front."

"Nobody did anything?"

The answer was that Keller was a priest. He had everything a molester needed: a vacation house that had room for exactly one less than the number he brought. The extra had to sleep with him. Boy or girl didn't matter. "He took the left over into the bedroom so they could sleep better," Helen was saying. "I know the priest had Bobby Schmidt in his room for the whole night. Bobby never talked about it. Keller never tried to bother me in Jersey. He got back here, he talked me into coming into the rectory after choir practice. We're alone in the office and he starts playing with my bra straps. I got up and got out of there."

Her friend Suzie Eder didn't believe any of the stories she had heard about him until they were on a bus trip to a Jersey amusement park. "On the way back, she saw him in the back of the bus having sex with a young girl she didn't know," Helen Wolf said. "She was too ashamed and embarrassed to look."

Later, he offered Suzie Eder, now seventeen, and Heidi Schmidt, nineteen, a weekend at his summer home. "He had a summer home in Jersey on a bay and all we had was hot sidewalks in Ridgewood," Suzie remembered. "I know, we should have remembered. Heidi was uncomfortable all weekend and could barely talk to me. When we got home, Heidi broke into uncontrollable tears. She said that Keller had assaulted her for the whole time we were in the house. I called Keller up. He said he was busy. I told him, 'I'm going to the cops if you don't see me.'

"When I saw him at a park, he said he hit on Heidi because he wouldn't be a priest forever. He said what he did with her was in the normal course of life and it wasn't any big deal."

She remembers Keller saying that he never bothered her because she was special.

They then heard that Keller had been assigned to St. Margaret's parish, in the next neighborhood over, Middle Village, where there was a large grammar school and both choirs and altar boys and therefore plenty of room for a priest, the celebrity of the neighborhood, to fall on somebody young. Helen Wolf complained. The diocese transferred Keller to St. Pancras in one neighborhood over, Glendale. He didn't do much good there.

In April 2002, with the papers filled with news of sexual aggression on minors out of Boston and Kentucky, despite his denials of abuse, Keller was taken off the roster in Brooklyn.

"I wonder where he is," Helen Wolf said over coffee after church. "I kept my mouth shut until 1995. How sad can you get?"

After this, I met Bobby Schmidt for coffee on 42nd Street, across from Grand Central. He is burly and balding and he says hello with a broad smile that gives no hint of the years in which his memory of being molested turned into a knife and left him wounded for months.

"My sister and I were walking on Forest Avenue up to Joe's Pizza by the library and she said she was just thinking about this Father Keller. She asked me if I'd ever had any trouble with him. I said, 'Why ask me?' She told me about Father Keller forcing himself on her. She said she told him, 'What do you think you're doing?' I got mad when she told me. I said I'm going to tell her right now. Right while we were walking to Joe's Pizza."

"What did you tell her?"

"What happened."

Abuse follows an established form, but the suffering is unique to each. The methods used by a priest to get at these young is out of the Middle Ages. Bobby Schmidt was a choirboy and an altar boy at St. Matthias all through grammar school. The moderator for both these groups was Father Brian Keller, who, according to Bobby and other witnesses, walked into each group, the choir up in the loft, the altar boys down in the basement, as if by his mere presence their young lives had meaning and gladness. He took these choirboys and altar boys on summer weekends to his shack in Jersey. Bob Schmidt, Sr., did not have money for things like that. According to Bobby, the roster of kids on the trip changed all the time in line with Keller's preferences.

"Then one time he had two kids I didn't know with him. They were a brother and sister from public school. They were in one room in Jersey. Keller sat on the bed next to me. He put his hand on my knee. I told him I was nervous about starting high school. Because we didn't have any money, I was going to have to go to a public high school. Franklin K. Lane. It was mostly black. I was afraid of that. He said he could get the church to pay for Cathedral Prep. That's where you used to go when you're thinking of becoming a priest. I was worried about public high school. It turned out I had a right to be. Sitting there that night I was very vulnerable because of my fears. When I went to sleep, he just got in bed with me and put his hand down the back of my pajamas and on my bottom."

He was silent for a few moments.

"That's the one thing I don't remember," he said. "My memory stops right there. I don't know if anything happened after that. I can't see it. My mind stops right there. I don't know how it ended."

They all complained. The diocese started transferring Keller. The transfers were being made under the administration of Thomas Daily, who once had been in Boston, where he moved the worst offenders into the parishes with the most children and once made a notation, "Problem: small children," and still transferred the priest.

On the corner of 69th Street and Myrtle Avenue in Glendale, in Queens, is the St. Pancras school. On Myrtle Avenue, there is a diner, banks and eyeglass stores and supermarkets and small clothing stores. Myrtle Avenue is crowded with delivery trucks and buses but the noise is surprisingly less than you would expect. Up 69th Street is St. Pancras. The sidewalk runs up to the church steps and alongside is a large lawn and a long walk leading up to the rectory. The street is as restful as the fresh green on the trees. A long time ago, after mass, the people I knew went around the corner to Mulligan's on Myrtle Avenue. All gone. We took Ray Ward, the bartender, to see the Mets at Shea Stadium and he had five hundred beers and thought he was watching the Yankees. He kept asking when Mantle was coming up.

I was married in that church on a cold day after Christmas long ago. The bride's name was Rosemary Dattolico, and I was in the church a couple of years later when her sister, Phyllis, was married to Donald Noonan.

I remember the mass for Private Gregory Ambrose, who was my friend Fat Thomas's favorite nephew. Gregory called me on the phone from Hong Kong in January of 1968 and gave me an overview of the war in Vietnam. "I have to get off now. I have a guest coming to the room." Big shot, at age twenty. He went back to Vietnam to finish his tour, which was to end in mid-March.

On the night before St. Patrick's Day, his stepfather's bar, Gibby's on Myrtle Avenue, was decorated with big welcome home signs. Two army officers walked in and told Gibby that Private Ambrose was dead in a war. At this hour that night, an Irish Night at St. Pancras ended just in time for Gregory's three sisters to start home in tears and with a dagger in every step, fainted, one after the other. Two young priests said the funeral mass at St. Pancras, but only the mother remembers the names.

And then on September 15, 2001, at a nuptial mass that was thrown into St. Pancras as if by pitchfork, old people with canes and walkers, the morning mass regulars, came to church, with the young streaming past them. The place was soon filled. Babies cried and small children sat thumping their feet against the kneelers.

The priest came on the altar to start the mass. No bride came down the aisle. No groom awaited her at the altar.

"They're not here yet?" a man asked a woman next to him.

"He's here," she said, pointing to a young man sitting alone in a pew in front. "She won't be." She was looking straight ahead, with rosary beads covering her hands. Now she said, "She worked at the Trade Center, ninety-third floor. She don't come home. There was forty people in her company. They're all missing. I don't know what company. I know they're missing. The whole lot."

"How old is she?"

"I think, thirty. They're looking all over for her," she said. "What's her name? Dianne Signer. I know the aunt. The family comes from Ridgewood. St. Matthias."

At the end of the mass, the fiancé, Paul Mauceri, got up and said he was sorry that there was no wedding and that he missed Dianne and prayed they would find her and he thanked the people for coming.

It was the first nuptial mass I ever heard of that was held without a bride.

It was also the first time that people in St. Pancras could recall a woman dying in war and leaving the man mourning. Through the wars the neighborhood knew, World War II, Korea, Vietnam, the man always died and the woman carried the flag home from the cemetery. Now the woman dies and the man holds a mass for her. People wondered if this would be the way of the new war.

And in this same parish was damage done by religion that I never saw or heard of before. I met a woman named Jane Burke, who, at seventy-six, was standing on the stoop of her house on 70th Street in Glendale in the morning, tapping the mail that had just been delivered into the palm of one hand and performing the main duty of chief block inspector. Looking. She lives in an attached frame house of two stories and an attic and tan siding. Mrs. Jane Burke is a mother of eight, a parishioner at St. Pancras. She had three sons attending St. Pancras in the sixties who were altar boys and were molested by one priest, Father John Sickler. She lived in a wilderness unnoticed by anybody on the block. The church gave her the down payment for a house and paid all tuitions and some clothes. "A house and tuitions for sodomy, that was the tradeoff," daughter Barbara Samide says, unhappily. Father Sickler is dead.

There are twins, age fifty-four. Shane, a former high school principal, is now a Franciscan brother and the head of the order in Brooklyn. His brother John dropped out of a Franciscan novitiate and is a mathematics teacher at All Hallows High School in the Bronx. Both were molested.

Another set of twins are Barbara Samide and Brian Burke, age thirty-six. She was principal of the Catholic grammar school of St. Elizabeth's in Ozone Park. She has accused "the pastor of St. Elizabeth's, Father John Thompson, of molesting her. Thompson had also stolen money from the school." Barbara's twin brother, Brian, is a sergeant on the Rockville Centre, Long Island, police department. No one molests him. When he removed his jacket at a family party in a restaurant, he had on his right hip a Glock handgun that appeared large enough for war duty.

One daughter is a nun, Karen Burke, who teaches at St. Joseph's College in Brooklyn. Another, Jayne Burke, is a lay teacher at a Catholic grammar school in Manhattan. There is one bartender, Glenn, of A. J. Kenny's Saloon on Grand Avenue in Maspeth in Queens. Another brother, Kevin Burke, works for the state as a sex crimes investigator.

John Burke and Shane Burke are homosexual. Diversity in Queens is now next door.

This Glendale family started when the mother married Martin Burke when he got out of the army in 1945. She was a Presbyterian, and a marriage of mixed religions could not be performed in church. They were married in the rectory. The priest said a white dress would be too billowing for the rectory. She wore a white suit.

Her husband was a truck driver for Canada Dry and worked weekends as a bartender and did some odd work as a policy numbers runner. Even with that, the money was tight. They lived in rent on 69th Place, the next block from St. Pancras.

In the middle grades, twins Shane and John became favorites of Father James Sickler. He came to the house for dinner. He took the boys out to dinner. He showed the father, Gerard Burke, how to make a Rob Roy. "Oh, God, the priest coming to the house, it was like . . ." Jane Burke, remembering this, waved a hand over her head. God.

The priest had a large cape for an overcoat and the boys told Jane Burke that the priest liked to have one of them come under the cape while they were walking. "They told me that he would say, 'Whose turn is it under the cape now?' " Jane Burke says. Then more and more, term by term, she says she sensed that there was something the matter. But, then, how could there be? How could there be trouble with a priest?

One night John came home upset. The mother remembers him breaking down. "I can't do what he wanted. He's a priest. I can't do what he wanted."

He had been in a car with Sickler, who demanded sex and, when denied, threw John out of the car along the shoreline in Canarsie. It was a long walk home, miles and miles, and he sobbed all the way home. He broke down completely the moment he got home.

The father went to the kitchen and came out with a large carving knife.

"I'll kill him," the mother remembers him saying.

The mother shrieked. John's brother had to grab the father. As did another brother. Then Jane Burke called St. Pancras and told a priest what had happened. He came running to the house. "He told us, 'Please keep this quiet. Something will be done right away. But please keep this quiet. These things happen,' " the mother remembers him saying. She remembers her husband on the bed crying.

A priest, not from the parish, obviously a messenger to keep the danger of lawsuits down, gave Jane Burke a $2,500 down payment on the house where she now lives on 70th Street. The church also paid for first communion clothes and high school tuitions for John and Brian, and their sister, Barbara. The money was the tradeoff for sodomy kept secret. One son, John, attempted suicide twice.

Now Jane Burke and daughter Barbara Samide and some of the family were in the first floor hallway of Queens criminal court to see Father Thompson sentenced for grand larceny. The molesting was in a civil suit that would come up later.

"Do you want to go in and sit down?" the mother was asked. She has light brown hair and was wearing a green pants suit. Barbara Samide was in a brown plaid shirt with the collar spread over her navy blue blazer. She wore a tan skirt. Her hair was short and light and her blue eyes are engaging. Her son, Andrew, ten, was with her. Light-haired, solemn in shirt and tie.

"I'm just going to stay here. I want him to see me when he comes in and I want to see him," Jane Burke said. "I've waited this long."

She and her daughter stood at the courtroom door and talked for almost an hour about the family. This time, the silence the church had tried to buy was replaced by the loudest of all operas, an angry woman. Barbara Samide, as plaintiff, witness, avenger, looked like a college student in her blazer and brown plaid, but she really stormed into the case banging on a drum. Besides going to the district attorney and then suing for the molesting, she wrote two letters

about her case to the diocesan officials in Brooklyn that were neatly
typed and in sedate language. The letters were designed to blow up
in your face. She had copies of them in a black leather looseleaf file
of her case. I borrowed the file and went into the courtroom and sat
down in the empty room and read the letters.

October 20, 2002
TO: Monsignor Otto Garcia, Vice Counsel, Diocese of Brooklyn.

A few weeks ago, my sister Karen Burke, C.S.J., had the oppor-
tunity to speak to Bishop Daily regarding the slanderous tactics
being used by diocesan officials to impugn my reputation and that
of members of my family. Bishop Daily clearly indicated to Sister
Karen that he does not approve of any retaliation . . . yet these
tactics continue to be employed . . .

The diocesan lawyers have accused me of stealing from St.
Elizabeth school and contacting parents in an attempt to hurt my
beloved school's reputation . . . While I was principal, Father John
Thompson invited me to attend a Mass he was celebrating on a
Sunday evening in Manhattan. Since my husband works nights,
the only way I could oblige Father John was to bring my seven-
year-old son Andrew. I did not know at the time that this Mass was
not in accord with the teachings of our church nor did I know it
was sponsored by the Defenders group [a gay club that wore
leather] to which Father John belongs. I attended this mass because, as principal, my pastor and employer requested me to do so.
I had no reason to believe beforehand that this was inappropriate.

Why is my reputation being questioned when in attendance at
this Defender's liturgy were two other diocesan priests from
Brooklyn, a Holy Cross brother from the school's office, and at
least one priest from the Diocese of Rockville Centre. The priests
from our diocese were Father Lavin from Park Slope and Father

Lynch from Our Lady of Lourdes. The priest from Rockville Centre was Father Mundy. Brother Clifford was also present. Father John introduced me to two of them. One was wearing the Defenders insignia on his clothing.

I find Mr. Cea's tactics toward me both un-Christian and slanderous. I am also deeply distressed by the slanderous lies being made about my brother, Brother Shane Burke, O.S.M.F., and my brother, John Burke. My brother Shane has been in consecrated life for almost 37 years. He is a devout man and humble man who has been highly successful in Catholic education. Brother Shane is presently the principal of St. Anthony's High School on Long Island. Recently, disparaging remarks have been made about my brother's bout with alcohol nine years ago. At that time, Shane was principal of St. Joseph's High School in Bridgeport, Ct. My brother Shane was very close friends with Cardinal Edward Egan, who was at that time Bishop of Bridgeport. My brother was having trouble with my father's death in 1993, and Cardinal Egan gave him pastoral and personal assistance with his struggle. Cardinal Egan traveled all the way to Queens in April of 1993 to attend my father's wake and funeral. My brother and Cardinal Egan became very close personal friends as Shane was often invited to the Cardinal's residence for dinner, and for trips to Oak Park, Ill. to visit the Cardinal's family. The relationship ended in an unfortunate manner and out of anger Cardinal Egan removed the Third Order Franciscan Brothers from Saint Joseph's High School and the Bridgeport Diocese.

My brother John's sexual identity was personally affirmed and supported by Brooklyn Bishop Francis Mugavero. John and our former bishop were also very close friends as my brother frequently ate dinner with Bishop Mugavero at the Rifle Club on weekend evenings. Occasionally, Bishop Mugavero would go back to my brother's apartment on 14th Street in Stuyvesant Town. My brother John also vacationed on the island of Saint Maarten with Bishop Mugavero at his residence.

December 28, 2002

Dear Bishop Daily,

On October 18 and 28 I wrote to Monsignor Otto Garcia of my serious concerns regarding malicious tactics being used by diocesan lawyer Richard Cea to malign the good name of my family . . . I have just completed a 90 question set of interrogatories sent by Mr. Cea. It is my understanding that, as the plaintiff in a civil suit, I am mandated to answer these questions.

Your Excellency, I know that you know the Burkes from Glendale personally, but I would like to share with you a bit about my family. My mother and father have been registered parishioners at St. Pancras for over 50 years. I come from a family of eight brothers and sisters and truly Saint Pancras was our home . . . Today my seven-year-old son is in the second grade at Saint Pancras. My mother and father gave three of their children to consecrated life to serve in the Church they loved so much. Five of us work in Catholic education.

My two older brothers, Shane and John are twins. Sadly, in the early 1960s while altar boys at Saint Pancras, Father James Steckler molested them. My brother John was abused by Father Steckler from 1960 until 1968. My father informed Reverend Joseph Weber, our cousin, and the diocese sent Father Steckler to Saint Rose of Lima.

My brothers went on to enter the Franciscan Novitiate. Shane was the stronger personality and seems to have been able to handle the trauma as he has been in consecrated life for almost 37 years. My brother John received a leave after one year to discern his vocation. John met Bishop Mugavero's nephew, Donald Kramer, in the novitiate and they became domestic partners. Bishop Mugavero and his companion, Msgr. Walker, were very kind and generous to my brother. They helped to furnish his apartment and took him on trips to the Bishop's condo in Saint Maarten.

Sincerely, Mrs. Barbara Burke-Samide.
October 28, 2002

I finished reading just before Thompson's case was called in the afternoon. He was an innocuous-looking man with pale hair and glasses. The judge was named Grosso. "This is an emotionally charged case," he said. "I don't want any outcry. If anybody does they will get thirty days on the spot. I'm a practicing Catholic and a daily communicant." He sure was Queens. He asked Thompson and his lawyers to come forward.

Thompson stood in his mildness. He looked as if past performances were misprints. I had pages of notes from reporting about that.

Barbara Samide had told me that one night, new to her job, she had driven him on her way home from a Futures in Education dinner at the Waldorf-Astoria to a Greenwich Village club called The Lure.

It was Defender's Night for Catholic priests. "This is an L and L night, leather or Levi's," she said he explained, and he was afraid that they wouldn't let him in dressed as he was. He got out, announced he hoped he wouldn't be home tonight, and headed for the bar with a pocketful of money.

It went on like this for two years. Pastor Thompson had told parents to pay tuition in cash to him because checks were too much trouble. His sister-in-law helped him collect the money. When he moved a young man into his room in the rectory, he verbally abused Samide when she brought this up. She could not handle his taking $14,000 brought in by pupils who sold candy bars.

My notes and memory show that on a bright warm June day, I am standing in front of the St. Elizabeth's grammar school and there are women squalling and waving their arms.

Schoolchildren came out without final report cards. The principal had been told not to give report cards to anyone who hadn't paid tuition in full for the term. Mrs. Ana Beltran's daughter, Destiny, in second grade, emerged empty handed, "I didn't get my report card," Destiny said. "You didn't pay the tuition." She said it casually. Being broke, behind in bills is not a great tragedy on these streets.

"Yes, we did," Ana Beltran said. In one of the jeans pockets she had seven receipts, with all payments paid in cash, as Father Thompson had asked. They added up to $3,200—the cost of tuition for the two children in St. Elizabeth's. Ana Beltran had one receipt for $376 paid in cash at the start of the school year. Pastor Thompson's computer entry showed a payment of twenty dollars. That's what got Thompson into court here today.

The judge said that Thompson had to make restitution of $95,000, of which $10,000 had to be put up now. Then he said that Thompson had an excellent pre-sentence report and that he had the gift of God—to consecrate bread and wine. "This is one of the toughest cases I've ever handled. How you can use the talents loaned to you. The church really needs good priests. You are an asset to the church. I sentence you to five years probation. Go in peace."

Somehow, a letter from an old, dear friend of mine was not in the judge's file. "It is time for John Thompson to pay back and he would be $300 richer if he did not buy those roller skates for my under age son without my permission and behind my back!"

It was good that the judge, being such a sensitive Catholic, didn't have to deal with the civil case against Thompson. The interrogatories for which were in a second folder of Barbara Samide's.

18. Plaintiff objects to this interrogatory on the grounds it is ambiguous. Without waving such objections, plaintiff nevertheless responds as follows:

Former employer and pastor John Thompson exposed his genitals to plaintiff and forced her to place his genitals in her mouth. This forced act of sodomy took place on two occasions, October 2, 2001 in the plaintiff's office and December 6, 2001 in the rectory of Saint Elizabeth.

Ringing in my ears is her sworn testimony that the pastor, John Thompson, was in her first floor office, intimidating her with his collar and title, and pushing her with his hands. He has the young woman in front of him as he sits and opens his pants.

She is disgusted by his pubic hair, dyed the same improbable blond as the hair on his head.

That she is a young woman causes many to immediately consider it as a lesser crime than a priest sodomizing an altar boy.

Then I was at the Courtyard Hotel across from LaGuardia Airport while then-Bishop Daily of Brooklyn was being deposed by Mitchell Garabedian, a lawyer from Boston. With Garabedian was his client, Patrick McSorley, who was suing because he had been abused by John Geoghan, who then was moved from parish to parish by Daily. At that time, eighteen years ago, Daily was in charge of personnel in Boston. He was greatly assisted by Bishop William Murphy. Daily was sent to Palm Beach, where he got out just in time to be clear of the town, for the next two bishops in a row had to resign. Daily was honored by being assigned to Brooklyn, where Catholics were counted by millions. His vicar, Otto Garcia, resumed the diocese's fifty-year policy of moving sex molesters from one parish to another as if they were errant patrolmen. Daily reveled in his position.

Murphy was awarded the rich Long Island diocese of Rockville Centre, where his efforts were devoted to his own comfort. His answer to sex abuse cases was to have the man put in a new parish and out of mind.

In a warm sun in front of the hotel, McSorley shivered. He spoke about his case in words bitten in half. Although the abuse had occurred so long ago, nearly two decades, it still attacked his mind. Back in Boston, they found him in Dorchester Bay on an apparent suicide try. Last February he died of an overdose or suicide in a North End apartment.

The statute of limitations runs out for molesters after five years from a victim's eighteenth birthday, or from the time of reporting the molesting to authorities. The times vary from state to state and in many places are now being changed by state legislatures because of attacks on the young by priests. A victim like McSorley lives in dread forever.

That there is an absence of cases in the last years, particularly cases that can be prosecuted within the statutes of limitations, has led many to believe that the abuse ended in the late 1960s when many priests left for marriage and those who remained outgrew desire. Which is another fine dream of things that never happened.

"You watch," Garabedian was saying. "Soon there will be another wave of victims. This thing never stopped. It takes so long for somebody to recognize what's bothering them. Then they have to get over the shame and report it."

It was only a couple of afternoons later that I saw this for myself. I was over at Herb Gardner's apartment on the East Side and we were talking in the late afternoon about his play on Broadway and then about the girlfriend of a philanderer who appeared at his deathbed right in front of his wife. Beautiful. Then Gardner began to talk about a high school teacher who had tried to assault him sexually. Herb did this from nowhere, for I had never discussed this Catholic project with him.

"He was teaching writing and that was what I wanted to do. He had me come over to his house. Only he could help me turn my writing into something lofty.

"The guy kept edging closer each time," Herb recalled. "One day it got nasty. I tried to shove him down a staircase. I had to get physical.

"He wrote me a letter in blood. He signed it in his own blood. He said he couldn't bear living without me. And that he could guide me to greatness as a writer. He wrote me in his own blood."

Herb seemed startled. "I've never mentioned this to anybody before now. What is it, forty-five, fifty years ago? I've kept it to myself. It's always been there. But this is the first time I ever talked about it. Isn't that something?

"The teacher was using the power of art. He was trying to subdue me with art. Think of the power a priest has over a young boy. The overwhelming power of a priest. A kid has no chance."

"And it bothers them forever?" I said.

"I've been living with it," he said.

Next, I woke up one morning to find a fax of a report by the Massachusetts State Attorney General left on the table next to me.

It read, "Bishop Daily had a clear preference for keeping priests who sexually abused children in pastoral ministry and generally followed a practice of transferring those priests without supervision or notification to new parishes rather than removing them . . . Bishop Daily apparently did not believe that a priest who engaged in such misconduct was apt to engage in such conduct in the future. Accordingly, he failed to take any meaningful steps to limit abusive priests' contact with children in the future."

About Murphy of Long Island, the same Massachusetts report said: ". . . And, even with undeniable information available to him on the risk of recidivism, Bishop Murphy continued to place a higher priority on preventing scandal and providing support to alleged abusers than on protecting children from sexual abuse."

Murphy is not in Long Island long enough to know the directions and he calls Linda Moraitis at her Farmingdale home one Sunday morning and tells her that he sees no reason to ban a priest whom she and her son testified had abused the son. "I told him he believed his priest and not my son," the mother said.

In Boston, Father Robert M. Burns arrived from Youngstown, Ohio, where he had been under treatment for sexually abusing the young. The bishop of Youngstown warned Boston that Burns shouldn't be near children. In Boston, you couldn't get him away from them. The man in charge in Boston, Bishop Thomas Daily, wrote in his own hand on Burns's record: "Problem: little children."

Yes, he did. Burns was transferred from one parish to another like a bus rider. There was a howl wherever he went.

Daily and Murphy both let a priest named John Geoghan slip into the lives of church families and leave them in pieces, one after another, endless ice cream, endless cooing, whose hands on the young might as well have held daggers for the maiming they did. Case report after case report states, "The subject wept when Father Geoghan inserted his penis into subject's anus. Geoghan told subject to be silent so that the mother wouldn't hear."

He molested hundreds. It is a dark surprise that he could ingratiate himself into the lives of so many families and children because people who saw much of him, who lived alongside him for years, knew him as a small, mean man.

Geoghan and his sister, Catherine, a schoolteacher, and his uncle, Monsignor Mark H. Keohane, a large Irish fascist, had a summer house on the ocean in Scituate, Massachusetts. Geoghan had shamrocks on the shutters and an Irish flag in front of the house. There were two cars and the license plates said, TRY GOD.

The three of them were on the beach all day, periodically running to the water to take the temperature and then writing it down on a chart. Geoghan then would come up to the children next door and show them the temperature chart.

For twenty years the Broderick family of ten children lived next door, and in Scituate that meant thirty feet between houses. John Broderick, now an investigator in Boston, remembers that no kid could pass Geoghan without his insisting that they speak to him: where were you going, what are you going to do there.

"He talks like Carol Channing and he always tried to edge a little closer and we just kept walking on," John Broderick was saying. "He was too interested in us. If we hit caps with rocks, he was all over us to watch."

The uncle, Monsignor Keohane, said mass at St. Mary's in Scituate until he took the pulpit one Sunday for an anti-Semitic and antiblack tirade of such wickedness that he was asked not to return. After that, he said mass on the front porch of the Geoghan house.

Geoghan had a frosted louvered glass enclosure around an outdoor shower beside his house. The Broderick outdoor shower was water, a shower cap, and air from the ocean. John Broderick recalls his father saying, "Take your showers outside. Take off your trunks and get the salt water off. No one cares. Go ahead."

In his wonderful spyhouse, Geoghan peeked through the louvers and watched ten bare kids take showers. "He must have gone insane in there looking at us," John Broderick says.

"He never got close enough to touch one of us because our father was always there," John says.

Geoghan and his sister insisted for weeks one summer, "We must have an ice cream party." They invited Broderick and a brother to the party at the Geoghans' West Roxbury home. The two boys arrived with their older sister, Beth, twenty, who thought she was just going to drop them off. She thought it would be a large kids party. Instead, dressed for guests at a dinner, with the table set, there was only Geoghan and his sister, Catherine. The kids were puzzled and uncomfortable. Beth Broderick knew that she was not going to leave. After the ice cream, Geoghan reached under the table and brought out a tape recorder. "Do you want to hear everything you said?" he asked the boys. He put on the tape and they thought it was nothing, and Geoghan was beside himself listening.

When they were older and the Broderick young had parties in the house in Scituate, Geoghan stormed in and saw them with beer and went home to call the police. Once, they were flying balsa wood model planes and one went through the phone wires and into Geoghan's porch. "You are trying to hit me with a missile," he said. "I have proof. Your fingerprints are on it." He called their mother. "Is this about those balsa wood planes?" she said. "Yes," he said. "Then we're through talking," she said.

One day a car pulled up at Geoghan's house and two Latino children were let out. The children went in Geoghan's house. The car left. "They were really young," John Broderick says.

It then went the way it had to.

"No victim ever hurt anybody," Maryetta Dussourd was saying of John Geoghan's prison cell murder. She sat on a bench in the Dudley transit terminal in Roxbury, speaking over the roar of buses. "No survivor wanted that. Survivors only wanted justice and our story told. Some kind of peace."

John Geoghan commited mass molestation in Maryetta Dussourd's house. He fell on her three boys and four nephews who were living with her. When questioned, Geoghan said, "It was only two families."

Now it was two days after the devil got into John Geoghan's

penitentiary cell with a shoe as a handle for a noose of socks. The devil was in the form of a perverted murderer named Druce. He put the noose around Geoghan's neck and turned the shoe end over end that tightened the noose to death.

It now was eight o'clock of a Saturday morning, and Maryetta Dussourd was on her way to work. She was in a bus terminal because that is how she gets to work. On the bus. Two buses, to be exact. When her refrigerator broke, she took a second job. The buses took her an hour and a half each way. She is in her late fifties, a light-haired woman with blue eyes. She had just gone into a Dunkin' Donuts that has no place to sit. Roxbury is of color; what are you supposed to do, give them tables and chairs like these other chain stores have for whites? She took a coffee container to this bench by the buses and talked between diesel roars. Her hand shook. "I get panic attacks," she said. Her job was somewhere around the corner. She won't say what it is. Some people come in weeping and embrace her. Others attack. "When John Geoghan died, we had people walking right into my job and saying it was my fault."

"My daughter called me at work," Maryetta Dussourd was saying. "She told me, 'John Geoghan is dead.' I said, 'Oh, my God. How did it happen?' She told me how. I said, 'Oh, I thought that he had security. This is terrible.' My daughter said, 'Mom, how could you worry?' "

John Geoghan walked out of the black smoke at the gates of hell with his collar turned around and his hands seemingly filled with ice-cream cones, but in whose fingers were razor blades, the better to maim all the young he pawed. He changed lures from ice cream to a stamp collection in the rectory of St. Andrew's in the Jamaica Plain neighborhood. He brought Frank Leary, thirteen, one of six children of a mother on public assistance, into the rectory to see the first Bulgarian special delivery. He wound up with his turned-around collar pushing the boy into a chair and them both saying prayers aloud until Geoghan stopped to have oral sex. A priest came into the room and broke it up. The boy never got over it.

Geoghan and his Roman collar roamed a short distance away to the dreary apartment of Maryetta Dussourd. She lived with her daughter and three sons, and four of their cousins. Geoghan came to them through the altar boys and Boy Scouts. Maryetta Dussourd, from strict Irish Catholic parents over here from Donegal, in Ireland, was happy to have a priest come into her house. Not only a needed man, a steadying influence, but a priest to save the souls!

Geoghan was taking one of the most direct routes for all predators: find me a single mother with no money and young kids, and all raised strictly in rural Catholicism, and I am a cheetah lighting on a three-legged antelope. The priest says, "Don't tell what I've done to you." The boy whispers, "Yes, Father."

Once he got into the house, Geoghan became a favorite relative, a nice uncle except that he went upstairs with the kids and had oral sex. Geoghan spent two years roaming Dussourd's house. He took the kids out for ice cream and then came home to their rooms to tuck them in with oral sex, and have them touch him. He brought one of the boys home to his mother's house in West Roxbury and abused the child in one bedroom while Geoghan's mother was in the next room. She announced in the morning that the noise of the kid crying had bothered her.

"It wasn't just the mother," Mitchell Garabedian, Mrs. Dussourd's lawyer, was saying. "He had kids in the house with his sister in the next room. She didn't know?"

When one of the boys collapsed at home and told Margaret Gallant, Maryetta Dussourd's sister, she wrote a letter in 1984 to Cardinal Law that could be the most glaring document, a medical report, on the deep sickness of this church. She wrote:

"There is a priest at St. Brendan's in Dorchester who has been known in the past to molest boys. The Cardinal"—before Law, there was Medeiros, now deceased, but whose actions seem at least suspect at all times—"had sent Father for treatments, and after returning to parish duties, he maintained a low profile for quite a while. Lately, however, he has been seen in the company of many boys, to the extent of dropping them off at their homes as late as nine-thirty at night.

"My heart is broken over the whole situation and it is a burden to my conscience since I am trying to keep a lid on the anger of family members, a very real fear of the disgrace this would bring the church, to all good priests and family and, finally, but most importantly, my fellow members to this Body of Christ who are left in the dark as to the danger their children are in, while I have knowledge of the truth."

He took that note, Cardinal Bernard Law did, and sat with Bishop Thomas Daily and did two things: they answered Margaret Gallant with a note that brazenly said absolutely nothing, and they transferred Geoghan to a parish called St. Julia's in Weston. He was all over the first boys he saw. Why Law and Daily were not charged with committing a criminal act is on a prosecutor's conscience. And there is a second question that waves dangerously over the church bosses like a snapped power line: were these two permitting Geoghan to maul more young boys because they were part of this, or did Geoghan have something on them?

Now, at the bus terminal in the morning, Maryetta Dussourd said, "The first thing the church did was have Father Thomas come and see me. He told me to forgive John Geoghan because I was a sinner, too. He said that if I kept going I would assassinate his career. He said I had to think of all the years he put in studying for the priesthood. I owed it to him.

"Then I went to what I was told would be a special meeting with the hierarchy. It was at the chancery and my two sisters had to hold me up. I don't know who was there. A cardinal or bishop in his red beanie. I remember being so frightened I didn't know. They tried to say that this was all our fault. Put it on us. I did get up three times and told them, 'That isn't so!'

"The archdiocese sent John Geoghan to Rome on a sabbatical. Then when the pope came to Boston, John Geoghan was right up on the stage. I don't know how he got the ticket. But I saw him on the stage."

The man representing the archdiocese, Thomas, now told Maryetta Dussourd that he had asked Geoghan if what had been said about his molesting these children was true and that's when Geoghan said, "Yeah, but it was only one family."

Maryetta remembers that with bitterness. "I called the *Globe.* I don't know who I talked to. He told me, 'That's not our story.' He said it was the *Herald's.* The *Herald* had been printing the scandal. So I called the *Herald.* The reporter told me, 'That's a big detailed story. I'll take notes and think about it.' I called him again a couple of weeks later. He said it was still too detailed for him. He gave me Mitch Garabedian's phone number. I saw him in his office. There were a couple of people there. I told my story and I was sure they were having trouble believing me. I said, thank you, and can I use your restroom. They showed me where in the hall. I went there and cried. When I came out, Mitch was standing in the hall. He said, 'We believe you.' "

Garabedian is a fifteen-round fighter. He could not wait to get into the same ring with all the purported power of the Boston Catholic church. He found it an illusion.

And one day at Maryetta Dussourd's house, there was Matt Carroll of the *Boston Globe.* The paper was putting a flotilla on the story.

With people like Kevin Cullen. His writing on Cardinal Law helped chase the guy out of his job. And now it was only a question of how much they would find out and how much damage it would do. The answer on both counts was a ton.

The day before this morning with Maryetta Dussourd in the bus terminal, I had flown from New York and was standing in front of the rectory, which is just behind the Holy Name church in West Roxbury, which sits high on lawns and steps like a shining jewel, of which the church admires so much. The pastor, George Carlson, had officiated at the funeral mass for John Geoghan. He was saying he had gone to Geoghan's house on news of his death to comfort the sister, Catherine Geoghan.

"There was just the two of us in the living room," he was saying, "and she had the answering machine on. There were four calls from your media. She didn't pick up and I could hear the voices. Not one of them offered a word of condolences. Pure business. I found it sad."

"How many of the brother's victims did she call and say she's sorry?" I said.

"Well, there's that," he said quietly.

"They're damaged a lot of years afterwards, too," I said.

"But still, four people calling . . ."

He was a mild, affable and handsome man with hair silver in the sun. I thought he stood for all of his church. Pleasant, reasonable, outwardly compassionate and with an ambition to last all his lifetime and leave his church for those to follow and all after that, on to another two thousand years. The church that will not give an inch. And the church that has no recognition of the horrors it has visited upon children.

Carlson made sure to tell me that he thought Bishop Thomas Daily was a wonderful man who would do anything for you. Daily was from the area, and of course had been in the Boston archdiocese. I knew that he sure would help the nearest child molester. I mentioned that to Carlson, but it went by.

At the bus terminal, a young woman came up and sat on a railing. Her name was Indira and she works with Dussourd. "Time for work," she said. As Maryetta got up to leave, she was asked, "What do you think of your church now?"

"We were at a demonstration in front of the Mission Church, the priest in his vestments shouted at us, 'You on the bullhorn. We're not like that. You lie. We're telling the truth.' "

"Do you go to church?"

"Only like that. To demonstrate."

"When was the last time you were in a church?"

"For my son's wedding. I can't remember when."

Then she stopped. "No, I was in there another time. I went in with my button. It said, 'Cardinal Law Preys.' I guess they knew I was coming in because they had the priest saying the mass come out and say how good it was to see me in church and he was glad I was back. Back? I looked up and down those aisles and I saw all the mothers with children and the pregnant women and I wanted to call out, 'Don't you know you're not safe here?' "

She shook her head and started walking. I went a few steps with her.

"If they ordained women, would that change things?" I asked her. Women are the center of everything I propose in any new parish.

She stared at me. "I never saw nuns come out for the victims and we were raised by them."

And that was that.

Then she said, just considering as she walked, "Sometimes I think that maybe I should go. Just sit with them and help them. I know so much and they don't. They could use me. I don't know. I think of it."

Mixed up between her religion and her church, but somehow it still is the place of Jesus Christ in whom she believes with all her damaged heart.

She walked out of the bus station and went to work.

I'm left standing in the exhaust, breathing steel. A cough, and an unexpected emotion.

Am I staying out of church and not attending mass to please myself? The coarser phrase for this is showing off. I have never regarded making myself known as a particularly tragic act. It has given me confidence to push much competition aside. So I can stride and shrug my shoulders and speak irreverently about the church. But even after all I've said and written, Maryetta Dussourd's speed of doubt was like water suddenly rising to soak a dry floor under me. Here is a woman, a stranger until now, a woman who is supposed to be a renegade of our faith, leaving me with a dagger in my confidence. Suddenly I know what I don't want to know, that every time I pass a church one part of me feels like going inside to the comfort of prayers and people and maybe a bank of candles playing against the dimness. Deny it if you can.

Simultaneously, I also believe that I'm not doing anybody any good by slinking back like some lost sheep matted with mud.

At meetings of the Voice of the Faithful in a hall in the Long Island town of Wyandanch, another in a church hall on 14th Street in Manhattan, and a third with several thousand attending at Fordham University, I spoke to people about trying a service in our own church building. All seemed enthusiastic. Nobody even mentioned cost. That was a fence I couldn't climb. You can't start opening up a church on your salary. Simultaneously, I don't know how to ask people to donate to something because every time I do, my past rules me. The only times I ever asked anybody for money was when I needed it for myself. Now when I ask people to donate for a cause I am certain that they think the money is for me and they have suspicious eyes as I speak.

Then I saw Eugene Kennedy again, at Fordham, and as he spoke I remembered everything about an afternoon when he came to our house in Forest Hills and said mass at the kitchen table for my late wife. I keep the scene with me forever. He magnified love, and needed no great cathedral to do it. Not even a small chapel.

I began to think about holding mass in kitchens and living rooms, then getting to churches someday. There is no question about small services happening somewhere, and soon. As you are reading this. When I mentioned mass in the house, the reaction went beyond enthusiasm: When do we start?

That is my dilemma in writing this book. I know I must attack this church that has let pedophiles flourish, the victims to suffer for decades and at all times to lie. Rome Rule is suffocating the American church. But my upbringing in this church that started at age four is not shucked off so simply, no matter what great hill of dark facts you gather. Your past prolongs indecision.

Such as the campaign to make Mother Teresa a saint, and quickly. So quickly that I felt it was to distract us all from the scandal of priests. Her sainthood could be a cheap trick. Mother Teresa was a sweet woman who started in Calcutta and wound up using the mayor's office in New York as a waiting room while police helicopters were summoned to take her wherever and whenever she wanted. When I hear her name I hear blades whirring in the sky.

She was a woman who came with the appearance of saintliness, and with a steel mace held under her habit.

At a Holy Cross College graduation where I was to speak, I am looking at Mother Teresa, who also was waiting to speak. Her face, framed by a white sari with blue trim, looked like an outline of Jesus

Christ. Her hands were clasped in prayer, the fingertips touching her chin.

"How am I going to follow this? She looks like the Lord and I look like a bartender."

I thought she might go out and tell the crowd that she had enough bread and fish to feed them all.

Since I saw her in person, even shook her hand, I began following the ascendancy of Mother Teresa, before and after her death in 1997. I tried to be objective about her stories. They gave her a Nobel Prize for work with the poorest in Calcutta. In her acceptance speech she said that abortion was "the greatest destroyer of peace." I pass on her politics. I do know that this put her right next to the pope. She went everywhere, even preaching against divorce in Ireland and then getting money from and extolling dictator Duvalier in Haiti.

Two miracles are needed for sainthood, usually with some cure. One miracle is required to beatify the nun, the step away from canonizing her. The first miracle credited to Mother Teresa was the case of a woman in India, Monica Besra, with a lump in her stomach said to be cancer. She placed a medallion of Mother Teresa on her stomach. The woman said that a magic ray came out of the medallion and the lump disappeared. This cured her cancer. The doctor in her town, Dangram, in Bengal, said there was no cancer tumor at all, that the bulge was from tuberculosis and it was cured by a year of medicine. Her husband, Seiku Murmu, said, "It is much ado about nothing. My wife was cured by doctors and not any miracle." Right away, nuns from Mother Teresa's Missionaries of Charity took all her medical records away. A rationalist group opened an "anti-superstition awareness program." The leader, Prabiir Ghosh, is known for exposing holy men who walk through dusty villages in India and fleece people by promising miracle cures, if the holy man only had your life savings to make the magic work. They didn't put

Mother Teresa in the same complete fraud class; she did nurse the sick and poor. But they would countenance no talk of miracles.

The Vatican said their doctors say the cure of cancer is true. Besides, the Vatican speaker said, we have eight hundred reports of Mother Teresa performing miracles. We just picked this one, he said. I would like to hear the ones he didn't advance.

If they beatify Mother Teresa and try to make her a saint, I name myself a bishop of my religion. And the way the fakes in Rome wave Mother Teresa's picture about as a true saint does nothing but cause suspicion about everything they say. How can you ever take these people seriously after they betrayed people who helped build the church here?

My Aunt Harriet is one of them. When Peter Arnone came back from the war, there was no place to live. Veterans lived in quonset huts, garages, in squalor in broken-down tenements, with their families. She and Peter lived in his mother's house in Long Beach and then in the house where Harriet came from, on 101st Avenue in Richmond Hill. In 1950, with three children, they were among the first to move into Levittown, built on flat former potato fields where a builder named Levitt put 17,500 homes, all alike, that started the new American suburbs.

The houses were called Cape Cods and had two bedrooms. It was the greatest housing bargain in the country. There was a $100 charge when the purchase papers were signed, and this was given back when the purchaser moved in. The cost of the house was $7,990. The monthly payments were $59. "That sounds like nothing but you have to remember in those days it was a strain to come up with that every month. The men weren't coming from jobs that let them save for a couple of years. They were coming from the army." Each house had a small apple tree planted in front. The tree grew and the attics became second floors. The houses, because they were cheap, were supposed to fall apart after some years. Not close.

Harriet Arnone sits in the same house she bought in 1950. The tree gives pleasant shade. The people were supposed to conform so much as to be lifeless. A young man who wanted to be a singer, Billy Joel, lived down the block from Harriet.

Peter Arnone worked in his father's furniture business, and she taught grammar school around the corner from the house. They had three children. He played golf on the Bethpage Black course.

At first they went to church in Hicksville, and then for some time the movie house in new Levittown was used on Sundays. "We were most concerned with having a parish that our kids could identify with. We weren't real until they had a place. I put twenty-five dollars into a collection for a new church, Holy Family. What a mistake that was."

All these years later, Peter had a stroke at age eighty-one. At the hospital, they found the circulation was gone in one leg, which they had to amputate. "Foxholes," she said bleakly. She went home from the hospital to an empty house. "Somebody should stay with you," she was told. "Oh, no, I like it here alone."

She had been on the floor for about twelve hours when a neighbor found her. She was in a coma and they put her in a ninth-floor room, one under her husband's. Upstairs, he was incoherent. Sometimes he would break out of it and ask for her.

Everyone who examined her said that she would die from the stroke at any moment, and even if she stayed on for a while, her life was effectively gone.

I went to see her a couple of times. The last time, I shouted at her closed eyes. The nurse gave a sad smile. I said a prayer and then kissed Harriet Arnone good-bye and told her that I loved her and then I left. I was sure that was the last time I would see her.

Peter Arnone's breathing stopped and he was gone.

He was not dead eight hours when she opened her eyes and said she wanted to eat. They had no idea of what to feed a ghost. They tried rice pudding. She announced that she wanted more. She fed herself.

On Saturday night, her three children, grown now, Harriet, Peter, and Paul, told her that her husband had died, They told her they would have a wake on Monday and a funeral on Tuesday morning.

So on Monday, she had nursing aides lift her into a wheelchair.

"I have to practice for my husband's funeral," she informed them.

She made it to the Holy Rosary church, where she sat with a pink rose and watched as they wheeled her husband's casket out. It was covered with an American flag, but her unclouded view from the right side of her face saw through the flag, the casket, and right down to the man she loved and lived with since 1941.

She went home to Levittown and raised the big American flag from the casket on the front lawn and sat in front of the house and tried to relearn how to read. Her daughter and two nieces who were schoolteachers came over to help.

Chapter Eleven

The pigeons of Seventh Avenue at noon of this day were dirty and brazen and accompanists to the start of a day of more cold distressing stories of the church. I wanted to duck them, but I could not. Father Frank Pizzarelli, who was in from Port Jefferson, out on Long Island, got off the train across the street at Penn Station and we went into a place for a hamburger and coffee. We talked about the death of Raymond Trypuc at age twenty-eight, and the reasons for his dying. The body should have been thrown onto the steps of St. Agnes Cathedral in Rockville Centre, the home of the Catholic church's Long Island diocese, which by now was close to having the oldest, most organized criminal conspiracy in the nation. Frank Pizzarelli, a large dark-haired man with a beard, talked of the death of Raymond Trypuc.

"He showed up in my teenage homeless shelter," Pizzarelli was saying. "I never knew him until I saw him. I don't know if we could have saved him. But the diocese committed the crime of giving him money when he was alone and had nobody to counsel him. It was like giving the poor guy a loaded gun to put in his mouth."

The wounding and eventual killing of Ray Trypuc started in 1978 when the parish priest, James Bergin of St. Francis de Sales in Patchogue, became what seemed to be a close, close friend of Trypuc's father, Raymond Trypuc, Sr. Trypuc was a telephone company lineman from eight to five and afterwards, he went right to a counterman's job in a delicatessen, where he finished at eleven at night. The priest slipped into his son's life in the hours when he was away. He took Raymond off on ski trips. "I'm working two jobs," the father said. "I can't do that for him." On the ski trips, the priest and Raymond were in one room. Certainly, the priest molested him. When a neighbor called the father and said he suspected Father Bergin, Trypuc made the priest come over to the house, where he admitted it. The next day, a nun called Trypuc and said the priest was off in therapy. At eighteen, Trypuc joined the army. He came home and money immediately was missing in the house, a sharper warning than lights at a railroad grade crossing. He tried drug rehabilitation on Long Island. Then he went to Father Pizzarelli's shelter, Hope House. "When we finally found out a priest had put this kid into trouble, we called the diocese. Placa was in charge."

Monsignor Alan Placa was a beefy, duplicitous man who was the vice chancellor of the diocese, putting him one step under a bishop. He was advertised as the closest friend, the spiritual adviser to Rudolph Giuliani and held himself out as a protector of children. He was also a lawyer who bought silence from victims in sexual abuse cases in the Long Island diocese.

The only person he couldn't save was himself. Placa came to the job with complaints of his sexual abuse of young men that went back to the steam engine, though he has denied all these accusations and has never been criminally charged. According to a grand jury report in one case, the young man helped Placa make banners for a parade protesting the *Roe v. Wade* decision and with the banner covering him, Placa fondled the boy's genitals. The report also stated that he tried to grope a young man in front of the casket at his father's wake. Placa, a priest named John Alesandro, and a third, Frank Caldwell, had a diocese intervention team, which meant they interviewed priests and victims and their families and settled the cases secretly with the victim's family and in many cases, priests were shuffled to another parish without a thought about the priest's next victims. What makes them so important all of a sudden? We don't even know who they are.

Placa had priests on his staff go to Pizzarelli's Hope House and remove Trypuc without Pizzarelli knowing it. Trypuc vanished into the sky and off to a rehabilitation facility in Arizona. He was in two facilities and then payments from the diocese ran out. He called Placa on Long Island. Placa sent him $25,000 to sign a release saying he would not sue. The money did not last long in the sun and drugs. Neither did Trypuc.

Placa tried to say that he had done the proper thing. "That was it for you?" Pizzarelli was asked.

"No. I said the funeral mass."

The molesting complaints about Placa caused his suspension as a priest. He went to work for Rudolph Giuliani's new company in Manhattan. He was allowed to say mass twice, and that was over the casket of Giuliani's mother and his own.

After seeing Pizzarelli, I had to go only a few blocks downtown to meet Tom Faye, who was in the Triple Crown Bar on Seventh Avenue. He was on his lunch break from working in the carpet business. He was there to talk about his son, who commited suicide on Long Island after being molested by a priest, he said.

"How did you lose the kid?" I said.

"I live in Holbrook," Faye said. "My wife and I were out buying patio furniture and when we got back to the house there was a police car in front. I figure, 'What are they here for? The kids broke somebody's window. No, around here, they won't call if that's all that happened. They know me and they know they'd get paid and the kids kept in the house.' "

"You didn't think of anything worse?"

"I just stopped thinking. I saw a neighbor standing outside his house and looking. I didn't like that, I guess. My wife was different. She gets out of the car and runs into the house screaming."

"She knew."

"I guess women do. I went to the neighbor and I said, 'Joe, what happened?' He said my kid fell. That's all he said. I went inside and he was on the floor. He died suddenly." He put his head down and said no more. He didn't have to.

"We went to the hospital," Faye said, "and they had him up on this stainless steel table. He was blue. I kissed him and left. You lose a son, fifteen years three months."

A priest, Father Brian McKeon, who was a very close friend of the young man's—"You'd like this priest as soon as he walks into the room"—had been out of town when Faye died, but he returned and served the mass and gave the eulogy.

"All I know is that he was there, our favorite priest, Father Brian McKeon, on March 2, 1987, says mass for my dead son. He immediately came around to comfort the youngest brother. He always was with us so much. Barbecues, golf, family outings. Then grieving. Once, I had this thought. He never hung out with a family where there was just a daughter."

One day, a little over two years ago, young men in the neighborhood fought over a priest's affections. Then some of the neighbors talked about McKeon, who has been identified in lawsuits as an abuser and has previously admitted to engaging in "inappropriate" conduct with young boys. After which a family friend, Bob Fernandez, a retired New York detective, called Faye's wife.

"Bob said to me, 'I wanted to tell you myself before you hear this from anybody else,' " she recalls. He told her that the priest McKeon had molested the dead son. Then the priest molested the second son.

Trypuc and his wife went to the Long Island diocese headquarters in Rockville Centre. They saw Monsignor Alan Placa, who did abuse complaints precisely as expected. He promised to investigate and report to the bishop.

On St. Patrick's Day 2001, Faye remembered, he and his wife were in Manhattan on 48th Street and 5th Avenue, watching the parade, when the Nassau County Police Emerald Society marched by with chaplain Brian McKeon out front. The Fayes couldn't get through the barricades. They went to Park Avenue and took a cab up to 68th Street. Faye ran back to Fifth Avenue in time to jump into the police contingent. He was in the rank right behind McKeon. He made McKeon step out of line and go into the park, but the place was filled with police. Faye left. "If you ever see him tell him I'm looking for him," he said to me now.

Faye had to go back to work. I started to go home, but a note scrawled on my notebook caused me to walk two blocks to Eighth Avenue and 23rd Street, where a dull red awning at number 332 West 23rd gave the name of Leo House. It is an eight-story stone building whose brochure notes, "is a safe, quiet guest house with a Christian atmosphere, centrally located within New York City, and is staffed by the Sisters of St. Agnes and lay persons."

There he was, in these years from 1995 to 1997, leaning over the front desk and greeting and booking all guests, most prominently the young: the Reverend Paul Shanley. All he had to do was step outside to be on the streets of the Chelsea neighborhood, teeming with young. There can be no realistic estimate of the number of young people he had attacked and abused in Boston. They stopped counting at only sixteen of his stadium full of victims.

He seduced a fifth-grade boy and kept abusing him for four years. The archdiocese paid $100,000. It was one of several settlements. The archbishop, Medeiros, did nothing. Shanley had a street mission, with the homeless young and drug addicts. He dressed counterculture style, with no collar and long hair. He ran schools and dances and special clubhouses. His life was an aberration, and nobody stopped it. In 1978, at a conference, he said that sex with children hurt nobody. He said the same thing in a magazine called *Gaysweek*. He extolled man–boy love. Medeiros received so many complaints that he had to revoke Shanley's street ministry. Shanley then made it known he had enough on Medeiros to turn the diocese upside down. In some sort of compromise, Shanley was transferred to a money parish in Newton, where nobody young was safe. He had no way of controlling himself and he went everywhere, walking into wards of hospitals, prison hospitals, a home for children. He was Catholicism's busiest pedophile. He had Bishops Daily and Murphy supposedly monitoring him. They did nothing but write letters praising him.

Finally, with too many complaints coming in, he moved, or fled, to California, where he ran a hotel for gay nudists in Palm Springs. He came back east and followed his close friend, Frank Pilecki, who had been the president of Westfield State College in Massachusetts until he went openly mad over young boys and got himself busted. Pilecki came down to run Leo House on 23rd Street. He went off to die, but left his gay connections to Leo House open for Shanley, who arrived in 1995 as a priest and assistant director.

It was a marvelous position. There were seven floors of rooms renting from sixty-five dollars to eighty-six dollars a night. The place is known everywhere in the world as fine lodgings for decent Catholics who need no bar in the lobby or ornate bedrooms.

His background was known. Neither the Boston nor New York archdiocese complained. There was an indictment looming in Boston. Shanley was still all right at Leo House.

And then somehow John O'Connor, archbishop of New York, happened to look at the Shanley file and saw the address of Leo House. West Twenty-third. That was right in the middle of Chelsea. In the political district of Tom Duane, then in the City Council. Tom Duane was gay and not reticent about it. And he was not quiet about O'Connor, who preached that being gay was to attempt to leap over the pit of the flames of hell and survive if you can. Why, if this Duane ever finds out about this Shanley!

"Get him out of this archdiocese now!" O'Connor thundered.

Never mind about all these hundreds of young people abused by Shanley, and as a result grew up with minds in pieces.

After me, they come first.

Shanley was gone to his fates with the Boston prosecutors and courts. He is in his early seventies so the flaming part of his life is over. His playing field is a cell with big thick bars. But it is an example, perhaps the most telling of all, as to the regard the church has for the helpless.

Chapter Twelve

At this time in this book that I am writing, the sky comes up in the morning and the first thing it does is fall on me. By now, there have been so many unnerving stories from Boston, Louisville, San Francisco, and New Orleans. They were the most evil accounts of the church, and when they first came up I skipped over them. I am supposed to love trouble as my living. Any imbecile can bring you good news. The task is to find something that can disturb and even hurt people and warn everybody about it. This might have been taking me far too long. I started with the *Baltimore Catechism* at age seven.

Q. Who made me?

A. God made me.

I am trying to write and I get a phone call from a woman whose son was sexually abused and now, even with the passing years, cannot recover. Or the mail in the office has a letter, a postcard about a rape. I am in the daily news business for so many years and I can handle all occurrences. Two mobsters shot in Brooklyn. I am out on the street. Breslin makes all editions.

Now it is another matter.

I want to report that my son was molested by the pastor.

I have a former altar boy in therapy because he was molested by the most popular priest in the parish.

I have two altar boys sodomized right in the sacristy by the pastor.

That bishop sat next to me while I played the piano and he put his hand into my pants.

Oh, don't worry, I made every run. But every call like these threw me for a day, two days, even more. There were new people to see, witnesses to ask, court papers to find.

And as it is everywhere else, from political government through large corporations and their near relative, big religion, disastrous flaws in one area mean you have them all through the organization.

Look at this, I said to myself, as I hunched over microfilm in the library and concentrated on old popular Catholic reading. On reel after reel here is the issue that Catholics don't talk about, but which still is so common that it impedes Catholics as surely as a broken leg: Jews.

I never understood how the blame for the crucifixion was shifted from the Romans, who did it all, to all the Jews, then and now. Roman rule and soldiers, using crown of thorns, hammer and nail, and by lance, by vinegar on a sponge, killed Christ. The campaign to put it on the Jews started at the foot of the Cross. The Romans cried, "Ammazzo Cristo!" Christ Killer. It is a phrase that has lasted longer than the aqueducts. It is one fire that nobody has put out for two thousand years.

At one moment, the present pope announced that the Jews should be forgiven for killing Christ. Beautiful. Let bygones be bygones. Then he announced that it seems like we shouldn't blame all the Jews all over the world for killing Christ. Then he even said we might think of apologizing to the Jews for what we have been putting them through for a couple of thousand years.

All in the first Crusades, in 1095, were supposed to free Jerusalem for Christians. The Crusaders painted crosses on their shields and galloped off for Christ. Of course they had to go into the

Rhineland first and cut Jews into strips. They left the descendants for the Nazis.

I suddenly realized that if I wanted to present prominently my reporting on the church, and let it help me take over a parish, crowning myself bishop and conducting religion based on the Life of Christ and not the splendor of a pope or cardinal, I would have to be our Camerlengo. He is the person who, upon a pope's demise, rushes into the room and pulls the pope's ring from his hand, and using a hammer that is centuries old, bangs the ring into pieces. Suddenly, I am the Camerlengo of my own parish and my hammer may not be ancient but it is relevant. I am going to smack the Irish. Always, a Catholic neighborhood in New York meant Irish. I must attack my own kind, because they can neither spell nor pronounce Ammazzo Cristo but still, now, today, they come into church wearing the word like a necktie.

Q. Where is the animosity highest against blacks and Jews?

A. In any decent Catholic neighborhood.

In all the years of growing up in my parish, there were two important papers for Catholics, the *Daily News* and *The Tablet,* a weekly published by the diocese of Brooklyn. The *News* had a circulation of over 2.5 million and ran color photos of British royalty and scathing editorials against labor unions, supposedly the *News* readers. These contradictions didn't cost the paper a copy. Not as long as the *News* comics had plots that were ahead of Einstein. The detective Dick Tracy, invented by Chester Gould, had the world's first crime laboratory and a two-way wristwatch radio. *Buck Rogers in the 25th Century,* long before Von Braun, flew into space with something called a rocket ship. Milton Caniff, the artist, became as famous as his strip, *Terry and the Pirates,* featuring the Dragon Lady. And Al Capp became a national name with Li'l Abner and Daisy Mae.

The city had three major-league baseball teams, and interest was so high that there were little crowds in front of candy stores at seven in the evening waiting for the early edition of the *News,* which carried the result, a short story, and agate type for play-by-play. Then in the morning, they bought the paper again for the full story on the game. The front of the paper had great divorce cases because of adultery, two dead bodies in Brooklyn, a young actress sitting on a baggage truck at Grand Central station, her skirt scandalous, after arriving on the *Chief* from Los Angeles, and scathing descriptions of blacks as savages and animals and welfare cheats.

The Tablet, which was sold by grammar-school kids, had makeup that duplicated *The New York Times* and copy that went beyond the *Daily News* in slandering blacks. *The Tablet* also protected fascism because it was surely going to take care of the Jews. They were communists, the natural enemies of *The Tablet.* The news rule seemed to be: Snarl about the blacks for a paragraph or so. Devote all remaining energy to the Jews.

The editor, Patrick Scanlan, wrote editorials such as this in August 1933.

Have you been reading the way in which our Jewish fellow countrymen are reacting toward conditions in Germany? Mass meetings, resolutions, boycott threats, protests in Washington. The press gives prominent and lengthy news space and carries strong editorials. Washington already asked for an explanation and State Legislatures are taking action. Very few accurate or authorized stories are presented, but even rumors, discredited reports or gossip are set forth for prominent space.

Thus The New York Times, *in a lengthy Monday morning story, presented its view of the atrocities:*

Seven Jews living in the Frankfurt district of the city were ordered to go to "barracks" in their district to undergo questioning. They inquired of police what they had to do and were advised to obey. At the barracks they were confronted with leveled revolvers and were compelled under threats of death to flog one another until several of the Jews lost consciousness. Among the victims was a father and son.

The whole story is indefinite, names are not supplied, time or location is not given. The charge, if any, is not presented. Then to climax the whole issue, the Times *writer stated, "It is impossible to verify their stories."*

When we attempt to launch a campaign of protest against the persecution of Catholics, the Jews lift their eyebrows as if we represented a group of a dozen longshoremen.

Page one, April 1, 1933:

BERLIN, March 28—Reports widespread abroad concerning the persecution of Jews in Germany are greatly exaggerated.

Unprejudiced observers with a normal sense of proportion report that very few disturbances have in fact occurred, and that where they did occur all were of minor matters of no serious importance.

Here is a *Tablet* domestic news short:

Officers of the Bergen Street house on Saturday raided a candy store at 1440 Flatbush Avenue and confiscated stacks of lewd and pornographic magazines. They were kept in the rear of the store and sold to minors.

The store owner, Mark Greenstein, was given a summons returnable in Magistrates Court on March 11.

The officers were James McGuinness and Arthur Stone.

Also sold by bright, scrubbed, combed schoolkids was the magazine *Social Justice,* which was published by Father Charles E. Coughlin of the Shrine of the Little Flower in Royal Oak, Michigan. He was known as the Radio Priest for his broadcasts that went to twice the number of people anybody gets today. Coughlin did it in a country half the size and with no portable radios, notes Charles R. Morris in his book, *American Catholic*, easily the best on the subject. You would hope that only nitwits listened to him. He once drew eighty thousand to Cleveland's Municipal Stadium to hear a speech that began, "we . . . believe in Christ's principle of Love Your Neighbor as Yourself, and . . . I challenge every Jew in this nation to tell me he does not believe in it!" His audience was so huge and his ambitions so ominous that when he began to consort with populist Huey Long of Louisiana, the Roosevelt White House welcomed Coughlin, for they saw him as serious political opposition. When Long was assassinated, Roosevelt dropped Coughlin.

The magazine had a soft cover with no pictures and school kids sold it in front of church, calling out, *"Social Justice!"*

My friend Alan Baker sold it for more money, in front of St. Aloysius Church and Doheny's bar on his street, West Side Avenue in Jersey City.

"You sold it for a quarter, a movie cost that much," Alan Baker remembers. "If you caught a bookmaker or a saloon keeper coming out of church he gave you a dollar and you gave him no change. Then at six o'clock everybody was home listening to his radio show. He was one hundred percent for Franklin Roosevelt. So was his audience. So he gave you our greatest political hero and then some good shots at the Jews. I remember people saying, 'He's not really for Hitler. It's a couple of the ideas he likes.' Then he did a stupid thing. He went against Roosevelt. Everybody stopped listening." Baker remembers, "They took him off the air and the magazine went out, too. It didn't matter. Once he turned on Roosevelt he was a rumor. Back to the rectory he went."

Coughlin began editing his magazine from an office halfway down the avenue of mental illness. He ran profiles of Young Hitler and Benito Mussolini. Late in the going, I brought one home and my mother glanced at it and said, "No." That ended it.

"I don't know how a religion based on the teachings of a simple man became so golden and theatrical and fearsome," my wife was saying.

Her name is Ronnie Eldridge and she is Jewish and has been looking over my shoulder and of that of every Catholic she knows for some time. She makes no cheap arguments. She was a politician elected four times to the City Council of New York. Instead of the thousand rules put down by both her temple and my church and mine over mixed marriages, she sees it as elementary politics. "Religions were conceived to ensure an orderly society," she was saying. "They are pure fantasy developed to explain the origins of humanity and provide hope for a future. Your Catholic church and philosophers brilliantly conceived the ultimate threat of hell. What better way to ensure obedience than to threaten people with eternal torture and suffering? Once they had hell established, power was centralized and the bureaucracy grew. As your church government grew, so did the perks and the quest for more power. That's why the rules to escape hell and get into heaven were increased. Then they filled the whole thing with mysticism."

She didn't advocate it to anybody. There was no proselytizing for an idea that she thought was this apparent. Certainly I threw in my answer. "You left out one thing. God." The Italians who followed the Irish did not have the language and took some time learning it. Believing Lincoln was the greatest American, many joined the Republican Party. During the construction of the Brooklyn Bridge, the Irish contractor fired Irish who were making three dollars a day and brought over boatloads of Sicilians whom he paid two dollars a day and told them to be on time and smile. On these ships were the advance brigades of the men's clubs of Palermo, the

Mafia and Unione Siciliano, which merged on the Lower East Side and began killing and bombing everybody between them and the money.

All these years later and John Gotti is playing cards in his club-house on 101st Avenue in Ozone Park, in Queens. It is called the Bergin Hunt and Fish. When he emerges from the club he can go to the right, a short couple of blocks, to St. Mary Gate of Heaven. Or he can go to the left, to Nativity. He chooses to stay in his clubhouse and rob both parishes. He concentrates on his hand. The priest from Nativity comes in. Gotti is paying the church rent for the parking lot, where he runs an outdoor carnival, an Atlantic City on asphalt. The carnival consists of two games where children could win a teddy bear or a baseball cap. And ten different kinds of wheels, dice games, and card games, all made legal by the seal of the Holy Roman Catholic Church. Walk on, policeman.

"Yeah," Gotti says, not looking up at the priest.

"I've been watching the receipts for the last couple of nights," the priest said. "I think I should get $25,000 more."

Gotti still does not look up from his cards. "Sal, do you know how to give the last rites?"

"No, John," the recording secretary, Sal Reale, answers.

"Anthony, do you?"

"What is it, like extreme unction?" Anthony asks.

"Yeah."

"I don't know nothin' like that."

"We better get somebody," Gotti says. "Because when I look up from these here cards and I see a priest, I am goin' to turn his collar around and kill the priest right here on the fuckin' floor and I don't want to do that if we can't give him the last rites."

Gotti put his cards down and looked up. The priest was gone.

This was over one hundred years since the Mafia opened up in New York. A century of slit throats, bullets in the brain, broken arms and girls squealing in delight in the night while riding around with gangsters in big fast cars. They are almost gone now. But for so long the Mafia was the disastrously colorful part of the Catholic church in New York. At the same time, the Mafia had the Sicilians, who might be the smartest of all immigrants, blocked and slandered.

The Irish used their numbers and the English language to have public success in the Democratic Party. The Ireland they left lived in the past and suffocated themselves with ancient tales of religious atrocities: "The worst thing to ever happen was when Owen Roe O'Neill died at Cavan while Cromwell massacred our people at Drogheda and Wexford." That was in 1650.

The Catholics here had their own school system, fiercely guarded by cardinals and bishops. Their people did not mingle in public-school schoolyards with these Jews. They were good Catholics. They obeyed. They never questioned anything. And right here is where the Catholics fell apart. The Jews from Eastern Europe began to scramble through public-school classrooms, one after the other, through excellent public-school elementary school and high school and then on to the great prizes of the immigrants, a seat at City College or Brooklyn College. Afterwards, to the graduate schools, medicine and law.

"Yes, sister," the Irish said. And in Brownsville, in Brooklyn, I. I. Rabi came home from school and his mother asked him, "Did you ask a good question today?" He kept asking and arguing until he was awarded the Nobel Prize for the MRI.

The earth changed in the late 1950s and '60s, with men of color up from the South walking the streets of Brooklyn with cotton baling hooks sticking out of their back pockets. They held sheets from real-estate offices directing them to houses that had apartments for rent.

They came to Catholic Brooklyn, and Catholic Brooklyn ran to Long Island and small suburban places such as Huntington, which had thirty thousand people, suddenly were metropolises of three hundred thousand.

Construction unions, which were heavily Irish Catholic, turned away every black face.

And the Jews, while hardly as enthusiastic as they claim, and not quite as a solid group, but still enough to form a movement, became the ones who identified with the needs and defense of the new blacks and had a tremendous moral and political triumph.

Writing about this, Daniel Patrick Moynihan saw that this left the Catholics off in their private-school system based on obedience. The Jews developed some rapport with blacks. The two got together and soon you could forget the Irish. The Jews were raised to argue and the Catholics to murmur yes. It was no contest.

In New York, in the 1970 race for statewide offices, the Democratic Party had a ticket of four Jews: Arthur Goldberg, Richard Ottinger, Adam Walinsky, and Arthur Levitt and one black, Basil Paterson, who was Catholic.

The State Democratic Chairman, John Burns, with powder burns from other encounters, came wearily to the back porch of Daniel O'Connell, of Albany, who was the strong voice of the state party. As Burns reported the ticket, O'Connell's hand went to the rope he felt pressing on his old throat and starting to strangle him.

"I never heard of anything so unbalanced in my life. What the hell were you thinking of?" O'Connell said.

"Well, Dan, Basil is a Catholic."

"In that respect he's the only white man you got on the ticket."

This church turned out such constricted people that the true Irish talent, being able to see the center of life and write about it brilliantly and lyrically, was made banal and unreadable by the years in the dull, hell-fearing classrooms. Sit with your hands clasped on the desk.

The Irish, who came out of the wet alleys of Dublin, and the creative mists of the bare mountains, put all their talents into writing insurance policies and traffic tickets in New York. They were left griping about all the Jews who were doctors and who took over the television and movie business. Few went to the corner store to buy *The New York Times* newspaper, as this was the Jew paper, that's all you read in it, anyway, the sands of the Sinai. The history of the *Times* newspaper is that during the Spanish-American War, while the two big papers, the *World* and the *Journal,* ran huge headlines and stories about raging battles in Cuba that did not exist, the *Times,* too poor to send reporters beyond Coney Island, used the Associated Press stories and that great I-beam of the country told the truth every day. The *Times* ran the AP stories with understated headlines. Soon, people found that the paper was trying hard to tell the truth. To show how greedy the owners were, they never stopped trying to give readers the truth and over the years it became apparent that they were often serving the country. The poor Irish were left with their *Daily News* that you now can't read.

For so long now, the Catholics identify science with Jews and in general don't want to touch sciences. Why would you want to study to be a doctor? The Jews have that wrapped up. Sell insurance! The Catholic mistrust of science shows in their high schools, which for decades had no science laboratories and many today are still inadequate. I have here the list of 2003 graduates from Regis High School in Manhattan. It is under the Jesuit order and has the reputation of being the top academic high school—religious, private, or public—in the city. Sixty-five of the 132 graduates have been accepted at Catholic colleges which are not known for science leading to medicine. Of the sixty-seven others, one is going to enroll at Massachusetts Institute of Technology and another at Worcester Polytechnic Institute. Otherwise, nobody touches science.

Then Catholics wail that there are no Catholic doctors because they're all Jews. Here we have the parish priest can't keep his hands off the altar boys and what can we do about it, send him to a Jew psychiatrist? This fear of mental help destroyed so many in the sex scandals. The priest wouldn't go. How can you blame him? He believes from earliest years that it is a custom of an alien world.

There was the morning that the mothers of a public school on Rockaway Boulevard in Queens reported that a car had been driving around the school, with the driver a male obviously trying to pick up a child.

I told this to my friend, Katherine Grunes, then an attending physician in the Bellevue Hospital psychiatric emergency room.

"Is that school in a rough area?" she asked.

"If they caught somebody trying to grab a kid on Rockaway Boulevard, it could get exciting," I said.

"It is very complicated to be out on the streets with such need," she said. "You could get killed. That explains priests being pedophiles. All you have to do is become a priest and you're in comfort and safety. And there are limitless opportunities to carry on sexually with children. A lot of these molesters have no desire for an older person. They want only children. So why not become a priest and be near children for what appears to be a legitimate reason? It's an addiction that is so one-sided. They knowingly damage another person. It is not sex as we know it. You have a threatened or tricked child or an older one, raped and terrified. Not one psychiatrist would say it was permissible for a priest to return to his duties. In fact, in my hospital, if a pedophile admits to you that he can't control his urges, I have him involuntarily admitted. If I am in my private office outside a hospital, my duty is to call the police. The man is not to leave my office. He is a danger to the community.

"That's why the prison sentences given to priests all have charges of kidnapping and assault to make sure they spend time in prison. Touching the genitals of a minor does not rate a long sentence.

"They should not be out," she was saying. "You can call it a disease or a perversion. Everybody knows that you shouldn't have sex with children. Anybody with an IQ high enough to discern that it is wrong to sexually molest children, knows it is wrong. If the urge is uncontrollable, then, knowing how wrong it is, they should turn themselves in. Everybody can go to a mental hospital. Just say, 'I'm going to molest a child if you don't put me in.' They have a choice: 'We can't help what we do, but what we do we know is wrong.' Seek help. Why do they plead not guilty? To get away with it. They know it is wrong but they still want to do it. When they are caught, then, they deserve little mercy."

She thought for a moment. "What about the seminaries where they go. What do they have to say?"

"There are not enough people in a seminary to talk to. I think they just ordained two people in the seminary in Huntington."

"Why is nobody in the seminary?" she said.

I murmured about today being different or something as deep.

"Because they're busted," she said. "They know that we know why they go there. So they don't go. 'It was a good place for us once. There's no sense in going now. They're on to us.' "

Chapter Thirteen

One New Year's Eve some years back, I was in the Margaret Hague Maternity Hospital in Jersey City, New Jersey, on the maternity floor to write about the firstborn of the New Year. There were nurses and attendants around something small and they had it covered and now an attendant was carrying it out. I looked at a sheet that said, "O.W."—out of wedlock. This kid had no shot at all, I told myself. Born wrong. No marriage. And dies without anybody to speak for the soul. So the baby goes to limbo. Limbo was the first belief of the church's Catholicism that I challenged. Limbo was the place where babies who died without being baptized were consigned. I don't know for how long. Half of forever, maybe for some baby who didn't even know she was alive.

Outside, I took a cab down to the subway for the Hudson Tubes in Journal Square and went down the alley to the Tube Bar, which is a busy dungeon and I sat in there and talked to myself about the dead baby. Consigned to someplace because she died before she was born? Impossible. Even mysticism sworn to and believed by all can't repel common sense.

I remember being far from Jersey City, in the garden at the North American College at the Vatican and a cardinal from Detroit, John Dearden, is talking about the meeting they had just had to choose a new pope. He said, "You could feel the Holy Ghost flying around that room." I thought this was a wondrous thing. I am talking to a man who has just been in the presence of the Holy Ghost. I could barely talk to him. Then as I was walking away, a natural emotion arose: What am I, a sucker? I guess I let the Holy Ghost remain in the air. Leave it to pleasant conjecture. But limbo for babies was gone. And that was the first time I took a belief of the Catholic church and threw it away.

We believed voodoo because it was tied to burning in hell, and hell was at the bottom of every day and act of the Catholics.

It was a mortal sin to eat meat on Friday, except if you lived in the far Southwest where they didn't have any good fish; eat steak in Tucson. If you were over sixty-five, then there were no restrictions because meat was good for the legs; it could keep you going. The Spanish, however, were allowed to eat meat on Friday. Real Spaniards from Spain. This was because they threw the Moors out. And they also ran a great inquisition. Catholics in the Philippines also could eat meat because they were part of Spain. This was changed by a deranged Methodist, President William McKinley, who ordered the islands invaded because God told him to do it. He then decided that the people were unfit for self-government and that America would just have to keep the islands. I don't know if this meant that people of the Philippines had to go back to fish on Friday or not. I do feel that the place is in the middle of the most water in the world and might find fish easy to catch and eat. Otherwise, everybody had to eat fish. Hell had its fiery arms open for all who ate meat and died without that mortal sin being absolved. Here's a guy burning for all of time for eating a lamb chop and he looks up from hell today and sees his cousin having steak on a Friday with church blessing. Does he feel robbed? Sure. What can he do about it? I don't know. I was taught that he went to hell and that is eternity.

You tell me I was crazy for believing it. What do you call the people who taught it? I was with my friend Bill Clark, an old detective who is now a television producer, in a place called The Old Stand on Third Avenue. He moonlighted as a bouncer there when he was a homicide detective in Queens and Brooklyn. Now he is the executive producer of *NYPD Blue* and is here on location for his show.

"I turned away from the Catholic church when they changed the rule on eating fish on Friday," he said. "If there was one thing that I thought separated us from everybody else it was that once a week, on Friday, we turned away from meat and ate fish. It was just something. A small sign. But we did it. And when I saw that they were ending this, and that they didn't care what we ate on Friday, then I gave them up."

"Do you think that people who ate meat went to hell?" I asked him.

"I don't know. All I know is that they changed the rules in the middle of the game and I don't play that way."

I told him about my idea to open our own group to worship in the Catholic religion, not the church.

"Only if you have real rules," he said.

"Fish on Friday."

"Of course."

"What if we were informal? We're going to be informal with most everything else. We could say, 'Let's all have tuna fish on Friday.' "

"That's lunch," Clark said.

"Dover sole," I said quickly.

He thought.

"Striped bass," I said.

"That could be good."

"Caught surf casting in Montauk. Big one. Twenty, thirty pounds. We would be the real Fishermen."

In grammar school, I believed everything completely, and so did every kid in class and all their brothers and sisters and all their parents, their parents stronger than anything the kids brought with them when they came out of the schoolyard at day's end. The trouble was, they had so much sin mixed with the goodness. Every time I approach somebody out on the street begging, I do exactly what the nuns taught, that we should give money to somebody on the street, even if they seemed fraudulent, for the act of giving was all that mattered. I never let go of this. Of course they drilled us on the Ten Commandments, although I always had a thought that you knew enough not to kill when you were born. You needed no stone tablet.

Purgatory was famous as a place of pain while you wait for people on earth to pray enough to have you lifted into heaven. It is a sure way to find out who your friends are.

There was one night when Al D'Amato, who used to be a senator, was saying to people at dinner, "I don't know what to do. I look at a priest now and I start to wonder. Is he all right? I don't think I'll ever be able to look at a priest again."

Then a guy I work with said, "I tell my kids, 'Don't ever be alone in a room with a priest.' I hear about this going in a room to confess. Never. I tell the kids, 'The priests don't have children, so they don't know how to behave with them. Be nice to them. But don't ever go into a room alone with them.' "

The center of the church is the eucharist, a white circular communion wafer that arises in unfathomable mystery from a chalice blazing with lights on its gold. On the darkest of early winter mornings, with sleet brushing the front doors like steel wire, even in the dimness of the last rows, the eucharist and chalice loom bright and promising and simultaneously ominous. The priest holds it high and announces, "This is my body, the bread of everlasting life . . ." He then holds up a glittering chalice of sacramental wine and announces, "This is my blood, the blood of the new and everlasting covenant . . ."

The congregation kneels in prayer and the altar boy rings small bells to highlight the powerful scene on the altar. They are small bells, but they become a rolling thunder.

This is the mystical transubstantiation, which they believe comes from Christ's own words at the Last Supper. The changing of wine and wafer into the body and blood of Christ. Of course the head must be bowed and the silence rules. He went from proclaiming these words at the Last Supper to pray in the dust and stones and be grabbed and crucified.

When the people line up and step to the altar, the priest holds up a wafer for each between his consecrated thumb and index finger, and says, "The body of Christ." They now allow laypeople, including women, to give out the communion. Their fingers are not holy, and therefore I always sidestepped their line during communion. Communicants either stand with open mouth as the priest places the wafer on the tongue, or they hold out their hands and then place it in the mouth to swallow walking back to their seat with head bowed and hands clasped. In the pew, they pray, frequently with face buried in hands. For worshippers, it is a moment of deepest reverence.

The sin that always demanded vengeance is to receive communion in the state of sin. The words confession and communion were as one. This pope of Rome demanded confession first. Forgiveness poured through the screen of the confessional and lightened the step all the way to the communion rail.

How are you going to go to confession now, with everybody on the other side of the screen a suspected sex molester? Or at least an accomplice because of their silence. Or, they sit face-to-face with you in a room and you're supposed to look at them and tell the sins you committed. Go somewhere else. And take confession or the sacrament of penance as it is called and scrub them from the rolls. Who are you, with your molesting, or knowing the guy next door is a predator, to dare think you can listen to my soul?

They have already destroyed the spirit of the religion and now they have put in doubt what we were raised to believe is most sacred.

The priest only touches the communion with his thumb and forefinger. These fingers hold the wafer as it is being turned into the body of Christ, as the liturgy says. Once, if a wafer fell to the floor, only the priest with his consecrated fingers could retrieve it.

Are these the fingers of a molester?

At the same time, running quietly through me is a creek of fear. By staring hard at the ceremony of the eucharist and saying, Priest, I do not believe what you say, then you could be denying Christ to his face.

It makes it harder to have good plans for my own church. How am I going to hold communion, which still must be the center of the mass? It is a mystery of the faith that reveals nothing through the mist. Certainly, so many other laws turn out to be the handiwork of dusty men in Rome.

But there is not much unknown about a dead body, including all shipping costs.

Chapter Fourteen

At this moment, Luis Milano is going to be buried on a promissory note. I am standing right over his casket in Chapel A of the Borinquen Funeral Home on Bushwick Avenue in Brooklyn. Milano is in an open casket in the front of the room and he faces mourners on folding chairs who don't have forty dollars to put him into the ground.

When the family came in to make the arrangements, the grandmother announced, "We have the plot. Thirty-five hundred on a burial policy. So we are all right."

"No, you're not," the funeral director, Sammy Lopez, said. "You still have to pay $1,300 to have the grave opened."

They all sat, defeated.

I'm here because I know Sammy Lopez for a long time and now I wanted to understand what he does. He stands in the doorway of Chapel A and says softly and gloomily of the deceased, "He had nothing. He was busted taking change out of a stolen car parked in the neighborhood."

I first met Sammy at a funeral for a man named Strange, who had died of AIDS or gunshot, I forget which, during the years of the eighties and nineties when bullets and dirty needles came through Bushwick like trucks. After prayers and hymn singing, Lopez stood in the doorway with the bill. The people went out the side door in one piece, like an airline cargo container. Lopez sighed and put the body in the back of the funeral home, in the refrigerated morgue. Someone would come, he was sure. Nobody did. For over two weeks. I stopped around and asked Sammy, "How is our man?"

Sammy said, "It is good I have a cooling system. He is doing fine." He turned to the body. "Good morning, sir."

Lopez kept the body on cold air. Finally, Sammy put the bill in his mouth and chewed it like gum while he packed the late Mr. Strange into a van and drove to Evergreen Cemetery where Sammy owned a plot. He had it opened for $1,300 and Strange put in.

The body this time was Milano, who died young and broke. Sammy was sure the family would not flee. They were going to sit here broke and let fate provide, if it could.

In the open casket, Milano, forty-two, who died in jail after serving a month of an eight-month sentence in Rikers Island, had on his Yankees cap and a good enough suit. His five children stared at his casket, desolate and in confusion. "His hat," a small boy said. He pointed to the cap. If his father had his Yankees cap on, then why wasn't he here with them?

The mother of the children, Milano's wife, was so stiff with grief that she couldn't get out of the chair.

The mother of Luis Milano, Elidia Ramos, wailed, "Two policies I have and they don't pay. Twenty years I pay the one policy. I call them up and say my son is dead and I would like the money. They say, no, you won't get money."

She was giving the correct reason. Insurance companies don't want to pay anybody for anything. And if you're a Latino or black, they usually won't even answer the phone. Think about it.

The wife said, "The second policy, too."

"Both times they steal from us," Elidia Ramos, the mother of the deceased, said. She said she bought the $5,000 second policy through a television commercial for an insurance company in Syracuse. A section of the policy was in type reserved for sports-page racetrack entries.

"I don't read it. It was so small it made my eyes hurt," Elidia Ramos, Milano's mother, said.

"He has to live two years from the start of the policy. He has to be alive October 10. Today is only September 18," she said.

She gave the start of a sob. "For two weeks."

"Three weeks," someone said.

"Two weeks, three weeks, what is the difference? Shouldn't they forget such a little thing?"

I'm in Bushwick to observe the burial business, and that's exactly what it is. The ground always earns. If money is absent, the dead hands are not yet so dead that they can't reach out from the casket and clutch your arm, insistently. You pay. That dead man now is a relative in need. By your presence, simply looking at his family, the deceased becomes a very close cousin.

Immediately, I went back to my office and called the insurance company in Syracuse. I was no longer an interested bystander. If they don't pay, some of the bill is mine. I thought for a moment that if I ever wound up with my own parish, funerals could put us on food stamps. You can make a lot of money on burials if you have many, many parishes. But going one at a time, with each time a chance of somebody being broke, is a danger you can see forever. I said to myself now, let me see what we can do with this insurance agency. The woman answering policy calls for the insurance company put me in shock. Instead of a cold "Sorry," she was a nice woman, and she said that if we got enough medical papers to her, she probably could have the policy paid. That would pay $1,300 for opening the grave.

Later, John Powis would call the Syracuse company. Yes, the woman confirmed, the family would be paid.

When he came to Bushwick in 1988, it was a time of shoveled

dirt for John Powis. The first two years of AIDS and gunfire in Bushwick, 1989 and 1990, started one morning when Powis, as new pastor, stood in the entrance to his church and looked for the casket he was to say mass over. The sidewalk was empty.

"Where is everybody?"

Luis, who is no relation to Luis in the Yankees cap, was from the parish and was going to help at the funeral mass. He shrugged.

"You'd think that somebody would be here," Powis said.

This was his first funeral at the church. He had no idea of how many would follow. Nobody did. Inside, the rows of empty pews ran together to the eye, the merging ending only at the front pew, where there were only a couple of old women, praying for the husbands who had gone before them. Powis was supposed to start a funeral at nine-thirty, which was now.

He stood on the steps and looked up to the corner San Juan Funeral home. The sidewalk was empty. He stepped back inside and waited.

Now from out on the street there was this squeaking sound. Suddenly, a casket on a rickety aluminum carriage was wheeled to the bottom of the church steps by two men from the funeral home.

Following was a woman, the mother, and a young guy, a brother or whatever. That was it.

The night before she had sat alone with the casket in a small chapel at the San Juan. It was the last night that would happen. After this, John Powis would be there. Now, going into church with the casket, she told Powis, "No maricon." Not gay. She imitated putting a needle into her arm. "AIDS," she murmured.

There was the young man in the casket and nobody to mourn with her for the son she had delivered and always loved and raised the best she could by herself. The father of course was nowhere to be found. In church now, she walked down to the front row, with the casket alongside her in the aisle, and she prayed and cried, and

John Powis tried to overcome the empty church with an intense funeral service.

He drove with her and the body in the undertaker's station wagon to the Fresh Pond crematory. Nobody had the $3,500 for a plot and $1,300 for the grave opening. They turned to fire. The mother went home with ashes.

The routine was similar to a factory job. At night he went to the wake, in the morning at nine-thirty he ran the mass and told families to live for the living and understand and pray for the poor young dead.

He had two funerals in one day. One day he had three funerals. He went on to serve at 450 funerals in two years.

At night he tried to sleep but could not. He worked his teeth and chewed on the insides of his cheeks until they throbbed in pain. His mouth was ripped and every night he ripped more of it. He got up with a hammer striking the top of his head. He knew he had a funeral to do. When he brushed his teeth, blood splattered all over the sink. He barely could get down his breakfast of orange juice, toast, and raisin bran flakes. He has never had coffee or tea.

For years, Catholics could not be cremated. Now they are allowed and the remains can be brought to the mass. The rulebook says that the scattering of ashes on the water or the ground does not show enough reverence for the dead. It is far better to bury the ashes in a family plot or in a niche of a tomb provided by the Catholic crematory.

These niches are the single largest source of income for the churches. The funeral services come to $1,200 or even more. The cremation costs $300. But the $300 worth of ashes now have to be put in a niche in a building built for them.

"It is not like a condominium," Lopez from Borinquen points out. "In a condominium the higher you go, the more it costs. But the lower your niche the higher the price."

The greatest spots are those shoulder high, so as you stand there your aunt's ashes are in front of your eyes. For $2,200.

You have a thousand shoulder-high niches, and the church then gets $2.2 million. That is, the church, the diocese, the big fat bishop, not the broken-down parish.

Ten thousand niches runs to over $20 million. That is only for the box seats. And that is not an overstatement of the amount of bodies. Because your church knows something that you haven't even realized, that nobody makes it all the way. And if you want to go first class, box seat, shoulder high, make sure you leave enough money.

If you go out broke, you leave an urn of ashes on a level so low that people with bad backs can't even see your name.

I was seven when my father left the house and I never saw him again. Then in 1974, the *Miami Herald* ran a story saying, "Rich Writer's Father Dies Penniless." They were wrong on the writer's cash. Today, I am still running fifth and trapped between horses. They were correct on the father: He was in the morgue at Jackson Memorial Hospital and was going to be buried in potter's field. They found him dead in bed in a cheap motel near the old Miami railroad station. His fingers were cigarette yellow. The landlady said he smoked cigarettes down so far that they burned his fingers but he had such poor circulation that he never felt much. He died with a paperback of my first novel, *The Gang That Couldn't Shoot Straight,* on the table alongside. Make sure that everybody sees what his son did to him. I don't even know what he looked like. He ran away and left me at age seven and now he wants me to feel sorry for him. I asked Frank Durkan of Paul O'Dwyer's law office to call Colgan, the undertaker in Brooklyn who had buried all the O'Dwyers, and ask him to get the body cremated right away in Miami.

I actually considered asking for a burial. Wasn't it a great sin to cremate? I didn't know anything different. Two days later, Colgan called Frank Durkan. "You said you wanted Mr. Breslin cremated right away. I couldn't find a Catholic undertaker on Sunday. So I hope he isn't upset that I gave the job to a Jewish undertaker."

The silence at those nine-thirty funeral masses at John Powis's church was broken only by sobs during the mass. Powis hated it. He called for prayers for the sick, dead, for every mother and for those separated from their families by being in prison. He is the only one I ever heard to mention the jailed, although the Blessed Beatitudes of St. Francis of Assisi called for blessing on those who visit prisoners.

He now told women at an eight o'clock mass how cold and lonely it was at the funerals. The women then came into the nine-thirty with hymn sheets and sat right behind the mourners and sang. They were open, expressive people and had no trouble singing together so loudly that their voices rose to the top of the enormous Mediterranean church, with its twenty-five stained glass windows.

That they were singing for people who had died of AIDS made their singing only more important. In Bushwick, disease is no secret. At first, they would sit in the funeral chapel and insist to all callers, "He did not die of AIDS." At twenty-seven, what caused it, yellow fever? Soon, there were so many AIDS deaths that it was silly to deny. Powis arrived at St. Barbara's in 1989 when the number of people at mass was down to two hundred, and they brought forth 168 AIDS deaths. This was when the drug AZT for the first stage, HIV positive, had first appeared and somebody took too much and collapsed and others didn't take it and only one in ten lived for three years. There seemed to be nothing to stop the blood of an HIV patient from turning death black with full AIDS. Later, AZT was mixed with other drugs and people lived, but with deep nausea from the drugs.

Nearly all those dying with AIDS in Bushwick had contracted it from sitting between garbage cans in an alley or a basement and going seconds or thirds on a needle that could shoot heroin into the veins.

Gays used condoms to keep them from death. But the Roman Catholic Church was opposed to gay sex and birth control and virtually claimed that this judgment was infallible. Die in plenty of approval.

The Roman Catholic Church was wildly opposed to a clean needle exchange.

A person with a damaged brain would know that clean needles might let somebody live. A man named Martinez ran a clean needle program on Broadway in Bushwick. It was shakily safe, but better than nothing.

"I don't know why," Powis says. "But I knew they would get strokes if I came out from the pulpit for a needle exchange at that time. I did the best I could with Martinez."

And so John Powis, in a parish that had five hundred deaths in the two years in the nineties stood with his caskets as a duty for his church, and his church leadership, Cardinal John O'Connor thundered from St. Patrick's Cathedral: "I would spend all my time nursing and holding the hand of a person dying with AIDS before I would let him have a needle or a contraceptive."

If you were to organize any religious group, from a storefront to an old church, a funeral is the first assignment. The opponent would be the Roman Catholic Church, which battles for every yard of dirt.

I was raised in the news business with stories by Bill O'Dwyer, who had been mayor of New York and now sat in an East Side apartment and told of Cardinal Spellman's breaking of a gravediggers' strike in 1949. Spellman marched seminarians with shovels on their shoulders into the Catholic cemetery in White Plains. Spellman waited for photographers and then put a shovel into the ground, with a pudgy little foot simulating effort. The picture went all over the world.

"I was in the office looking at the pictures in the paper," O'Dwyer was saying, "and Mike Quill was outside demanding that he be let in." Quill, the head of the Transport Workers Union, spoke in two brogues, one soft and understated for business and the other thick and colorful for the public events: "The judge can drop dead in his black robes," O'Dwyer went on. "I told the secretary to get him right away. Here came Michael. 'Oh, the *byes* are restless. They can't wait for a contract much longer.' I said, 'Michael. We'll talk about that later. First take a look at this picture. What do you think of it?' I give the paper to Quill. He looks at it. I know he loves that little foot on the shovel. Then he says, 'Looks to me like the poor sonofabitch won't get down very far.' "

Many can't rest on earth until they have a plot waiting for them. I met Gerry Toner when he came off a job on the *Queen Elizabeth 2* and went right to work as a waiter in Rockefeller Center. At Christmas in 1969, he sent money home to his mother in Belfast. She went right out and bought a grave with it. "I want to find a place I like," she wrote. "I'm going to be there a long time." She chose the Milltown cemetery at the top of the Falls Road. It had a lot of IRA people, and a view of the area.

Her son, Gerry Toner, wasn't here two years when he owned a couple of big saloons in New York. He felt no need for a plot, as he decided he was immortal. Then in the year 2002, upon having chest twinges in the morning, he made three calls. One was for a priest. Then the doctor and finally the Holy Rood cemetery near his house on Long Island. On the way to the doctor, he stopped off at the cemetery and bought four graves for eight thousand dollars. "It sleeps eight," he said. Which means eight grave openings at $1,300 an opening for a job that should cost $100 each time. You now are up to $18,000 for the sale. Gravestones can run five thousand. Maintenance is fifty dollars a month. "Let someone else worry about that," Toner said. Still, Toner shudders at the idea of cremation. "You go up in smoke. Nobody will ever remember you. Ever get your finger burned?"

My friend Norton Peppis, aka Pep, a famous gambler, who had a big bust-out saloon on Queens Boulevard, where I first made my way as a columnist, had an uncle leave him a plot in Cedar Grove cemetery in Queens. During a particularly draining day at Aqueduct, he sold shares in his plot to three people at the racetrack, so he could get home from the track and pay the band before the night began or they would not blow a note. He assured the purchasers that they could be buried atop each other. As coffins wiggle and move when underground, the alignment wouldn't last long. "You're next door in a month," he said.

My thought is that the Catholics could sell me a few plots to get me started.

Going to St. Barbara's on Christmas Eve, I got off the Myrtle Avenue el at Central Avenue—Powis could not conceive of me coming by any other means. This midnight mass at St. Barbara's was held at seven-thirty in the evening, I stood just inside the church doors and listened as a wonderful, loud, thrilling choir dressed in red sang in Latin, the first I had heard in so long.

> *Natum videte, regem angelorum*
> *Venite adoremus, venite adoremus . . .*

Powis's sermon consisted of telling them about Health Care Plus. He said, "It is a great state program and you'd be surprised how many people in poor neighborhoods don't know about it. I'm sure some of you aren't familiar with it. You must apply for it. The mother and the children will have health coverage when you apply.

Remember, it is Health Care Plus. It is a wonderful program." He then went over Health Care Plus again.

Then he said, "Let me tell you about the trip I took earlier today on the 6 train. I had to go way up in the Bronx for a funeral service. While I was on the train, two groups of people sitting on opposite sides of the car suddenly jumped up and began to hug each other. They were friends who hadn't seen each other in years. They were so happy to see each other. It was a wonderful scene. Then a woman got on and said that she had eight children and she was homeless. She needed help. Eight children and homeless. It was such an injustice to hear her. People in this city are living in beautiful homes and here is the woman with nothing. What is the matter with us. What kind of people are there in this city? What does the city government do? We will try to do something for this woman. But we have to help all the homeless or we can never face God."

Then he announced, "I want everyone here to come to communion."

He blessed the crowd with the general absolution for all the sins they ever committed and the pews emptied as people went to the altar for communion.

There was a special trip up the aisle by the ushers, who passed out red envelopes marked, "Fuel Collection." They were an installment on the winter fuel bill. He has spent all his adult life in parishes that were poor and up to ninety percent nonwhite and he has loved every day of it. He also knows that these red envelopes, a celebration of primary colors, never hurt when you ask people who barely had their own rent, maybe, to come up with more change.

When the mass was over, he was at the front doors, shaking hands and exchanging great smiles with the people as they left. Afterwards, Powis had cake and soda with his family, which was large, cheerful, and with a roomful of kids. They all sat at a large table in a dining room that Powis ordinarily uses as an office. He had a glass of orange juice and peeled a tangerine. The cake and cookies were too sweet for him and he drinks no coffee or tea. Somebody put two bottles of scotch on the table, and Powis said, "Who wants a shot?" Not him. Somebody poured a drink.

He got up when a large man in a rain jacket came in from the church, carrying the wicker collection basket. He went with the man to lock it up someplace. Right away, I thought of Joanne Chesimard and her group of .45s. When he came back to the table, I asked him, "Do you ever think of her?"

"I don't know if I think of her, but she's all right with me. She didn't do what she said she could do. She didn't blow my head off."

"Would you give her absolution?"

"Sure. I have no problem with that. You have to give people hope. You can't have anything based on fear. If you don't behave you'll die and go to hell. Look at it in a more merciful way. Absolve and pray that the person succeeds."

"When Kennedy was shot in Dallas," I said, "I saw the priest who gave the last rites talking to Jacqueline Kennedy in the emergency room. So I went around to his parish later on. Huber, his name was. He told me that Jacqueline was asking him if the last sacrament was valid because it was given to Kennedy after he had died on the table. Huber told me that he assured her it was good. 'You have two hours before the soul leaves the body,' he said."

Powis was looking at me without expression.

"Three people believed that," I said. "The priest, Jacqueline Kennedy, and Breslin. I know she did. She told me that a couple of years later. The priest said two hours and that's what she believed."

"Four hours," Powis said.

Chapter Fifteen

The red envelopes did pretty good for John Powis this time, a couple of them sailing through the sky to unexpected points.

You never know where money sleeps. After the Christmas Eve services, some days later, my friend, Ed Ward, who is an affordable housing specialist, said he wanted to show me a housing story involving the church in Rockville Centre. The town sits in splendor on the Long Island Railroad line, some forty minutes from Brooklyn and Manhattan. At this time, people called or wrote letters, many unsigned because they came from priests, about scandals in front of them daily in the church. These accusations turned out to be absolutely right. The letters you could rely on the most were in crayon. They came from priests who wanted to remain good and anonymous.

On the top floor of a restaurant on the station square was the old gang war headquarters of what was once the Profaci Mafia mob, which was in a Brooklyn battle with a group known as the Gallos. Both groups were misbehaving Catholics. The Profaci guys thought Rockville Centre was a place nobody from their Red Hook neighborhood would ever find. How could the Gallos, who lived in one building, 51 President Street, up from the docks, know the first thing about Rockville Centre? One of them, Crazy Joe Gallo, kept a lion in the basement of 51 President Street. He threw guys he didn't like down to the lion, like antelopes. Here in Rockville Centre the Profacis were upstairs in the restaurant with steak, scotch, machine guns, and benches for sleeping. They went on search-and-destroy missions to Brooklyn. Since then, this was thirty years ago, mobsters have restricted themselves to Brooklyn and only commuters of pretty good means come off the train.

But on the best day of stealing they ever had, mob guys could not envision taking things like Mansion Murphy did. In honor of Jesus Christ, William Murphy, the Bishop of Rockville Centre and all of Long Island, threw out a group of aging nuns from the four-story convent at St. Agnes Cathedral in Rockville Centre in order to make room for himself.

"You can make thirty-four apartments out of the building, and he wants the whole place for himself," Ed Ward was saying.

Which is why on the spot we decided that the name was Mansion Murphy and will be for all of his days.

When Ed Ward drove me up to the cathedral and the housing in Rockville Centre, I knew I had come upon an almost complete guide to Catholic arrogance. And a great comic character in Mansion Murphy, whose name sticks forever.

The stone convent is about a short block long and four stories high and has a covered veranda on which fifty people can sit and observe the lovely lawn that runs out to a street that sits empty and silent in front of the convent. There is a space of brilliant green lawn that runs up to the rectory next door, which is far enough away to make it look like it sits in the next town. On the other side of the rectory, again a good distance, sits the high and sparkling cathedral.

First, Ward and I went to the rear of the convent, where a priest with an Italian greyhound took no notice of us. There was a reverse hoe and other pieces of heavy equipment sitting in the late afternoon construction mud. There was a one-car garage already there under the convent. Now they were building an adjoining three-car garage. At the end of the convent there was a large excavation. "That's where they'll put the exhaust unit for the heating and air-conditioning units," Ward said. "They need a big one. Everything is big here."

Walking around, we observed that every door and window was being replaced. The fourth floor is a line of up and down windows. There are a couple of stained glass windows in the sparkling glass of the other rows.

Inside, the building was being renovated from floor to ceiling. A few months before this, there had been six elderly nuns left in the convent from what once was a group of thirty who taught at the grammar and high school. The high school is gone. Murphy moved the nuns out in favor of opulence. There were only six nuns left to move because virtually no young women or young men are entering religious life.

The amount spent on the job would be an embarrassment to anybody except a Catholic bishop and in particular Mansion Murphy. One thing he had no worry about was shame. He was devoid of that. The construction work he ordered was to cost $5 million, including the $1.6 million for placing gold plating on the pipes of the church organ.

Mansion Murphy has a corner of the third floor, a great big apartment that precisely fits his idea of how much splendor he should live in. The apartment should cost about five hundred thousand dollars. Next to this is a smallish but still gaudy apartment for his secretary. Murphy can clear his throat at night and the secretary comes flying in. "Yes, excellency." At the other end of the floor there is an apartment that is not quite as large as Mansion Murphy's, but plenty big enough. He called it the *cardinal's suite*. This meant that his benefactor, Cardinal Bernard Law, when chased out of Boston,

THE CHURCH THAT FORGOT CHRIST

could come down to Rockville Centre and lick his wounds in splendor.

Murphy has a marble bathroom, and he spent $120,000 on a Subzero refrigerator/freezer unit, a six-burner Viking professional stove, and an undercounter temperature-controlled wine storage cabinet that can hold fifty bottles. The champagne and white wine are kept on the top shelf at forty-five degrees and the red wine is kept at fifty-five degrees on the lower shelf.

Irish, even bishops, are not great at wine. I never heard anybody with an Irish name say, "I'm going to stop for a good glass of wine." Mansion Murphy, however, spent long years in Rome, where these Vatican people move in the toniest of Rome, and he fancies himself a wine connoisseur, a gourmet eater, and when he tucks that napkin in his starched collar, he is royalty with a knife and fork. He has turned into probably the best example of the late Paul O'Dwyer's admonition, "You can never let the Irish into the parlor. The poor fools believe it."

Murphy read stories about himself and told the people in his office, including a friend of mine from whom most of these details first came, "Don't worry about it. This will blow over. People think their bishop should have a residence."

A woman working for him, a poor wretch, wrote letters to the editors saying that the stories were all lies and that the bishop is going to live in the mansion, yes, but many diocesan offices also will be under the roof. Do not hold your breath.

Murphy hired a heavyweight public relations man, Howard Rubenstein, for what I'm told is at least two hundred fifty thousand dollars to make him look good after all the bad he's done. That figure is not out of line with what Murphy has them spending on a four-story building that could be used for thirty-four apartments, and a four-car garage to go with it.

He had no idea of why anybody would dare question him.

Why, he had no time for that. He had a mansion to finish and furnish.

In Mansion Murphy's mansion there is a dining room table with twelve upholstered seats. It is Murphy's ambition to have big dinner parties where he can tell eleven people about himself all at the same sitting.

In the sitting room he has two exquisite armchairs flanking a fireplace. Right away it was noted here that both chairs appeared equal to the task of absorbing a direct hit by a big bishop coming straight down.

However, some side to side swaying of the same avoirdupois could splinter the arms of the chairs.

Murphy explained to anybody who would dare question him that, "If it makes sense that I could be close to the cathedral, which is my cathedral, then I should be."

He then announced his pleasure at having such a place to live. "It is fitting that the bishop of the sixth largest diocese in the nation should live like a bishop."

Soon, the mansion's front was a symbol of his living. There were nine new and expensive porch chairs on the veranda and they sat under chain lamps. The deck chairs were arranged so there was a middle chair that was flanked by four on either side. This was so Bishop Murphy could sit in the middle of a lovely spring evening and toast his friends and tell after-dinner stories about himself. There are park lights on the front lawn, which seems as big as the sheep meadow in Central Park.

At the base of the veranda wall are large vents that signal the size of the laundry in the basement. It is probably large enough to keep a county in fresh clothes. Also back there in the basement there has to be a billiards room or maybe a small theater for showing films.

In the rear, the garage for four cars was finished. Christ walked on foot. In his honor, Bishop Murphy uses cars. At the end of the building the exhaust for air and heat conditioning is big and well set in and it is behind a chain-link fence. The rude mechanical appearance is almost totally obscured by bushes. Alighting from one of his four cars in the garage, the bishop is cool in summer and warm in winter as he returns to his mansion.

By a Dumpster were two flattened cardboard boxes with a label saying they were from the Midwest Folding Products, Saugus International Company, quality built since 1947. I believe it was the rich brass screen that could go in front of Mansion Murphy's fireplace.

Mansion Murphy, in the diocesan office building a half block away, read this in the newspaper and went insane.

"Is the delivery here yet?" Mansion Murphy said. He had a big one coming.

"I'll look over in the mansion," a minion said.

"No. They're not to be delivered to the mansion. I ordered them delivered here in the lobby."

So that day, the first huge boxes of china and great good glasses were delivered to the lobby of his office building.

"We'll keep them here and take them over at night," he ordered. The bishop declared that Breslin would be looking for a delivery truck. Mansion Murphy had the first of his china and glasses moved at night by car from the office building to the mansion, two blocks away.

I compared Mansion Murphy to John Powis's red envelopes for fuel and I said that anybody who gives money to Bishop Murphy's church is crazy. And anybody in Bushwick who doesn't give whatever they can to pay for the fuel bill is no help in a storm.

Some days later, John Powis mentioned to me in a confidential tone, "Some people from Rockville Centre sent us checks." I loved to hear it. "How much?" He said, "Some of them were pretty big."

For St. Barbara's a fifty-dollar check is major financing so I had no idea of what he meant by big. Until one day I received a call from a woman in Westbury, Long Island, and she asked me if I thought the thousand-dollar check she sent to Father Powis got there. She was a lovely suburban woman of great conscience and tolerance, but I think she still was afraid that they would kill the mailman in Bushwick.

Now, with the news filled with his living arrangements, Mansion Murphy went to the whip. That was abortion. The churches in the diocese began to hand out new literature about abortions and rail against it in sermons. If ten percent of the people in the pews cared about abortions anymore, that was a lot.

At this time, the church everywhere began to cry abortion. Few people were aware that an effort was being made. This was because the church didn't have enough resolve over abortions to stir coffee.

"His name was Monsignor Re," my friend Mario Cuomo was saying one day. "Giovanni Re. He wasn't a monsignor long. Now he's a cardinal in charge of all the bishops in the world. He has a clean shot at becoming pope. I went to see him in the Vatican," Cuomo said. "I had an interpreter and he had one. He hands me the catechism with the page opened to the passage on abortion. I read it. Then he hands me the pope's personal book on abortion. 'Would you read this, too?' I said, of course. I read it. Now he says, 'finito.' He hands the books to his assistant. "He says, 'Basta per il aborto.' Enough of abortion. He wasn't being cynical. He had done what he was supposed to do. Fobo. That means clever and just near to cunning. Then he leans forward and says, 'Now tell me about the church in America.' I tell him that it is bad. Now we could start talking."

Chapter Sixteen

I wrote a couple of letters to Murphy," the man next to me said. "You should see what he wrote back."

"How can I do that?"

"I'll fax them to you later on."

His name was Robert Byrnes. He is a retired college professor and now teaches a couple of economics courses at Suffolk County Community College. We were standing along the wall at the first meeting of the Long Island chapter of Voice of the Faithful. This is an organization that was spanking new. It began in the Boston suburbs when small groups of Catholics, disgusted with their church, began to meet in order to produce changes. At first, there were only forty or fifty in a basement. The cardinal said they couldn't use church halls because they were against the church. They were. They wanted him out, first. So they had forty-five hundred in a hotel hall and Law was as good as gone. As the idea was stronger than a church belfrey, it spread here to Long Island. There was a crowd of about seven hundred fifty, which is immense for the suburbs, We were in a bare public hall in the town of Wyandanch, which is the poorest part of the suburbs. Bushwick in the suburbs. Murphy had refused to allow the Voice of the Faithful to meet in one of the Catholic churches the people own. He also ordered that no priests were to attend the meeting.

There were priests and nuns present.

The letters from Byrnes arrived by fax as promised and gave a written record of just how deep the megalomania has gone into this one bishop and from what can be seen, probably all of them.

Robert Byrnes wrote on May 22, 2002 to Bishop Murphy.

Dear Bishop Murphy,

I would like to respectfully repose these questions . . .

1. What is the cost of the third floor renovation of the convent?

2. Are there rooms available to you in the rectory?

3. Is there a house available in Rockville Centre for your use as a residence?

4. Are there no meeting rooms available to you in the Chancery Building on Sunrise Highway?

5. Who approves major expenditures such as these?

Very respectfully,
Robert Byrnes

June 5, 2002

Dear Mr. Byrnes:

I am in receipt of your letter of May 22nd concerning the renovation on the existing convent. I am providing you with an article which appeared in the *Rockville Centre Herald* along with a letter written by the Director of Public Information for the Diocese of Rockville Centre, Mrs. Joanne C. Novarro.

The house in which I am currently living will be sold and the proceeds from that will be applied to the cost of my moving into a residence next to the Cathedral and across the street from the Chancery, where the Bishop belongs. Trust me that the money realized from the sale of the house will be more than adequate to cover the cost of this move which is justified by both my role as your bishop and by my desire to be near my cathedral and my office.

Further questions such as the ones you have raised are certainly improper for a Catholic to raise to his bishop.

With my prayers and best wishes, I am

Murphy signed his name in pen.

June 15, 2002

Dear Bishop Murphy:

Your letter clearly responded to my question regarding the Diocesan house on Columbia Road. I was somewhat puzzled and, frankly, offended that you considered my other questions to be improper for a Catholic to raise to his Bishop.

Assuming you believe the renovations for your quarters and the expenses involved in these renovations are appropriate, I do not understand why you not only will not share that information publicly but believe that you should not even be questioned by a Catholic about such matters. It seems to me that now more than at any other time, secrecy is inappropriate.

To be admonished by my bishop for respectfully asking what I believe to be very proper questions, leads me to believe that your model of Church is one that assumes all Catholics will expect no accountability from their bishop in terms of finances and in fact, considers such expectations to be improper.

Once again, I respectfully request answers to the following questions:

1. What is the cost of the third floor renovation of the convent?

2. Are there rooms available to you in the rectory?

3. Who approves major expenditures such as these?

July 25, 2002

Dear Bishop Murphy:

On June 15, 2002, I responded to your letter of June 5. These correspondences followed previous correspondences between you and me.

Along with objecting to your comment about improper questions posed by me, I respectfully repeated my request for answers to these three questions.

1. What is the cost of the 3rd floor renovation of the convent?

2. Are there rooms available to you in the rectory?

3. Who approves major expenditures such as these?

Since I have not received a reply to my letter of June 15 in over a month, I respectfully request for answers to my three questions.

August 1, 2002

Dear Mr. Byrnes:

I am in receipt of your letter of July 25. You are correct. I did not respond to your other questions because I considered them inappropriate. For your information, I already had written to the priests of this diocese and explained to them the fact that the cost of providing me with a residence that is adequate for my role as the Bishop of the sixth largest diocese of the country is being covered by the sale of the house in which I currently live; a house that is not adequate for the work that I have to carry on as your Bishop.

Frankly, most bishops in my position would not have replied to your letter. However, I wish to always give to every member of the Church the benefit of the doubt, and I presume that you have asked these questions in good faith and not out of either idle curiosity or disrepect for your Bishop.

With my prayers and best wishes, I am . . .

August 5, 2002

Dear Bishop Murphy, I am in receipt of your letter of Aug. 1st. I certainly appreciate your willingness to continue our correspondence.

You have made it clear that you have no intention of answering my questions regarding the 3rd floor convent renovation, the availability of space in the rectory and the financial approval procedures.

I am disappointed that in a Diocese committed to openness and accountability, you refuse to share this information, other than that the cost will be adequately covered by the sale of the house in which you currently reside. Being somewhat aware of real estate values in Rockville Centre, I would certainly hope that the proceeds of the sale would more than cover the cost of your new quarters.

Be assured that my questions were not posed out of idle curiosity or in any way to disrespect you. On the contrary, these questions, which you characterize as inappropriate, were asked in an attempt on my part to ascertain the cost of a Diocesan expense, to explore other possibilities and to understand the methodology by which diocesan expenditure decisions are made.

I respectfully submit such questions are entirely appropriate. It would seem to me, that in a spirit of openness and accountability, all diocesan income and expenses should be available to members of the diocese. For the time being at least, it appears this is not to be so.

Again, thank you for responding to my inquiries.

Very respectfully,
Robert F. Byrnes

Aug. 27, 03

Dear Bishop Murphy: . . . You have made it clear that you have no intention of answering my questions regarding the third floor convent renovations, the availability of space in the rectory and financial approval procedures.

I am disappointed that in a Diocese committed to openness and accountability, you refuse to share this information, other than that the cost will be adequately covered by the sale of the house in which you currently reside. Being somewhat aware of real estate values in Rockville Centre, I would certainly hope that the proceeds of the sale would more than cover the cost of your new quarters. Should I receive no reply to this letter within the next four weeks, I will assume you have decided to ignore me and not reply.

Very respectfully

Just printing the name Mansion Murphy in a paper caused his cash register to get stuck. He had his famous Bishop's Appeal set at $15 million. At first, his office admitted that it was down thirty-four percent and later even more so that if he wound up with half the appeal it was a considerable score. Next year, as more charges and stories and trials occur, the money could go even lower. He will throw one dinner party at his residence and reporters will be all over it and my name for him, Mansion Murphy, will appear in cement in front of his residence.

And he is still Mansion Murphy and people have stopped donating money and that levels him out pretty soon.

Chapter Seventeen

The town of Oyster Bay is on the North Shore of Long Island and juts into Long Island Sound. It is wealth dipping a foot into the water. I am here because my friend Jack Lang, with whom I worked on newspapers for more years than seems possible, wrote me about a story that appeared about the Reverend Michael Hands, who had pled guilty to sodomizing a young boy. "This guy was my parish priest who said my wife's funeral mass," Lang wrote. The investigation caused by Hands went into the riches of Long Island. It is the one most protected sphere of the Catholic church: the money people who require no services other than performing marriages and funerals and graciously accepting a special donation to pray directly to God to get the person a guarantee to heaven no matter how sleazy the life that has been led. Wherever there are Catholics in the country, the ones with money are treated as the spinal column of the church. Oyster Bay stands for them all.

At this part of the rich Nassau County north shore, an estate is a common address. Oyster Bay itself is a town of one-story shops dressed for quaint. People who work for a living live in houses in town. The surrounding lands are in another universe, on estates of five acres, and this is only right because they have horses to graze. The town is separated into two social zones that for many come together at their church, St. Dominic's. First, on a corner, is a large, low modern church. Behind it is a brick grammar school of three hundred pupils, whose families pay $2,800 per year. The opposite corner is taken up by the old church, a gray stone church, called The Chapel. Then there is a large wood rectory and after that, on both sides of the street, sitting like a college campus, are the buildings of St. Dominic's High School. A sign on the front of one building proclaimed that the class of 2002 had an average SAT score of 1100 and that ninety-nine percent of the class went to college, with the top sixty-five students receiving $5.1 million in scholarships. The high school at last count had 515 students and tuition for parishioners was $5,380 and for nonparishioners it was $5,880. Computer Associates gave the school thirty acres for athletic fields nearby.

It is the grasping ambition of the old Catholic bishops and cardinals of the 1920s, who wanted to separate their people from the heathens and give themselves great power by building schools for children, that let them just about own these children through graduation, marriage, and life right to the grave. The ambition was as Irish as rain. Their idea of diversity was to ride two stops on the subway. The hierarchy's vision was the perfect corner of their past in the Bronx, at 138th Street and Willis Avenue. On the four corners were St. Jerome's church and grammar school, across from that a drugstore, then on the two corners across the street you had a police station and a bar. Every possible need was accommodated.

The buildings of St. Dominic's are the capital of the Catholic suburbs. St. Dominic's is heavily Italian, but they could not carry such splendor without the large contributors from the estates, the Dolans, Quicks, Wangs, Sbarros, whose checks add up to millions.

The church has 160 employees and an $8 million budget. In the 2002 Bishop's Appeal, which brings in the money for Mansion Murphy, St. Dominic's families gave an average of $466, which was the highest in the diocese. The formula for St. Dominic's provided for thirty percent of the money collected for the bishop to be returned to the parish. Don't hang from a cliff until he comes up with the money.

On the wall as you entered the church was a framed picture of Monsignor Bud Ribaudo, pastor since 1987. Alongside it should be at least a small snapshot of the Reverend Michael Hands. Bud Ribaudo could bring in the money. No rich man went untouched. Ribaudo was suspended from his priestly duties after charges against him for sexual abuse were revealed in a grand jury report. Bud Ribaudo, at sixty-three, was most comfortable among the rich. You can have the dreary poor. He will take the rich because he knows that playing with them leaves no dirt on your hands. All checks are on clean paper. He played golf with the best people at the Creek Club, a place that was founded on the idea that Italians were good at cutting grass, after which they should be banished from sight so as not to disturb a decent man's concentration on his shots. Ribaudo not only played at the Creek, but he held clubhouse luncheons on Wednesdays that only the favored attended. He sure got the money—at any hour.

A story in *Newsday* on Friday, April 5, 2002, said, "In an unprecedented move, the Suffolk County district attorney's office plans to empanel a special grand jury to investigate sexual abuse allegations against priests . . . The complaints [against Monsignor Charles 'Bud' Ribaudo] were made by the Rev. Michael Hands."

Ribaudo had Father Hands as youth director, whatever that meant. He and Ribaudo had known each other since Hands was a freshman and Ribaudo the chaplain counselor at Holy Trinity High School in nearby Hicksville.

On Sunday, April 7, 2002, he got up on that altar, Monsignor Bud Ribaudo did, and with all his heart denied the charges of sexual abuse. Ribaudo spoke at the family mass, 9 A.M., and told the crowd that the trappings of his heart, the ventricals and aorta, had let him down. The unseen, mysterious part of his heart that cannot be seen, the place from which the mists of goodness enter the blood, was more intense than ever. He had needed three open chest surgeries, including two quadruple bypasses, and two stents placed in his heart. That adds up to a lot of bypasses. He also denied the allegations made by Father Michael Hands of sexual abuse that Hands says took place twenty and more years ago. He said he sent in a letter of resignation on March 12 and didn't tell them about it. He did not say that he had resigned in advance of a grand jury report that he knew was coming up shortly. Yes, on March 27, he was stripped of his priestly powers. But this was not his problem. It was the heart, he said.

He had been in their homes, he had married them and baptized their children and buried their old. How could he molest a child? He left gallantly, and was promptly lugged away to a psychiatric home.

It turns out that the official word from the church decreed that Ribaudo had no idea of what his sexual orientation was. He really didn't do anything wrong sexually because he didn't know right from wrong. The diocese knew this for years and in one lengthy discussion and evaluation he admitted that he had abused at least twelve boys. He was not even admonished. "He had the art of seducing teenage boys down to a science," the grand jury report said.

The bishop and the rich parish did not want Ribaudo out. Sure, they could bring him back. The problem was this Michael Hands, the young priest whom Ribaudo brought around. If they could get Hands to tell a couple of decent lies, then Ribaudo could be right back earning money for the diocese. Of course Ribaudo is a desperately dangerous man. But there is something far worse: not enough cash.

However, Hands testified in a grand jury for four hours. Hands had criminal charges against him in Suffolk and Nassau Counties. He is the one who said too much about Ribaudo.

Here, in Hands's own words, is the single, solitary best description of the way the Catholic church does business. You don't know Hands. Neither did I when this started. But I did know Mafia bugs and tapes and reading court wiretap transcripts. This transcript shows that the inside of the Catholic church is just about the same as anything heard on a bug in any Mafia clubhouse. If you want to know the Catholic church, then read Hands. This is not a small suburban parish. It deals with Long Island, the sixth largest diocese in the nation and close to the richest.

Monsignor Hands had molested a then thirteen-year-old boy. Hands also charged that the Reverend Bud Ribaudo of St. Dominic's in Oyster Bay sexually abused him when he was in high school. Hands pled guilty to abusing the thirteen-year-old boy, in Suffolk County. The boy's mother sounded like city streets. Her advice to the Suffolk County district attorney about easing her complaint against her church was, "Eff them!"

Then Hands offered to provide a deposition on everything he knew. In turn for which Hughes's mother would not get up in court and scream to the skies if his sentence was not as long as she wanted. Simultaneously, the deposition would help in her civil suit against the church. She agreed.

The Reverend Hands is hardly heroic. The parents of the boy report that as a result of the molestation, and Hands's claiming it was consensual, they walked into the boy's bedroom just in time to find him standing on a chair with a rope around his neck.

The diocese told Hands that normally, if they had time before the complainant got to the police, they would settle with the family right away. There was no chance now. Hands stood in the way of clearing Ribaudo. Who was Hands to use some alleged high school dalliance to keep our Bud Ribaudo from continuing to live in the pockets of the rich? Is Hands's mind still in chaos? His duty was to save the big earner for the bishop. If he would keep his mouth shut about Ribaudo, Hands would be more sacred than cows in Calcutta.

Carol Eisenberg, a reporter from the newspaper *Newsday,* had heard about Ribaudo. She called about the story. The head of priest personnel in the Long Island diocese, the Rev. Frank Caldwell, went to Hands. The following is from a pretrial deposition.

"You know Carol Eisenberg, don't you?"

"Yes."

"Why don't you call her and tell her that Ribaudo had to leave because of heart trouble? Tell her this abuse story with you is an outright lie. Go ahead. We won't forget this."

Here is Hands's sworn statement about this: the "Q" is the molested boy's attorney Michael Dowd. The "A" the Reverend Hands.

Q. Tell me about the contents of those conversations with Monsignor Caldwell [the Bishop's secretary].

A. He visited me in St. Luke's Institute in Maryland when he was down for the bishop's conference. We talked for about forty-five minutes to an hour. I was extremely forthright with my conversation about what had happened with [the boy]. During therapy, after about two and a half, three months I had begun to remember and recall and speak about, for the first time, what had happened between father Bud Ribaudo and myself . . . The first thing Monsignor Caldwell told me hurt me. He said that he heard about these allegations I made about Monsignor Ribaudo and that it was sad because he had heard that Bud Ribaudo was such a talented man and that he had gone for psychological testing on Long Island.

Caldwell told me that they wanted to send Monsignor Ribaudo to St. Luke's Institute and I said I kind of have a problem with that if I would be sharing a facility together with the man I'm accusing of sexually abusing me. Caldwell tried two or three times to have me not oppose sending Ribaudo there because he thought this was good.

I tried to pretend that none of this was happening. I found from St. Luke's that they had firmly opposed his coming.

Q. Tell me about Murphy's conversation.

A. Bishop Murphy told me that before he came to our diocese he was working as a bishop up in the Boston archdiocese and he had handled many situations like this before, that I need not feel like I can't talk to him. He says that he heard it all before and that he understands, and that I could tell him anything and that he is not beyond handling such sexually explicit news. So I did. I told him everything. And at the end of the conversation I asked him for his blessing . . . I then had conversations with him via Frank Caldwell [bishop's secretary] in between.

Hands said that Caldwell was surprised when he didn't ask about Ribaudo and Hands said, "I don't care what happened to Bud, that's your business, and I hope you deal with that . . . And however you deal with that, I don't want to talk about Bud Ribaudo or anything about Bud Ribaudo."

Caldwell said there had never been a diocesan priest who has been psychologically evaluated as intensely as Bud Ribaudo. This was meant to show Hands that his charges were being handled seriously.

Hands then said that he had told the story of how Bud Ribaudo had touched him.

Q. (by Caldwell) This was what month, what year?

A. August of 2001.

This caused a certain amount of wobbling due to suddenly weakened knees. Caldwell checked the date when Hands had been arrested for molesting the teenage boy. That was in May of 2001. Three months after that Hands talked to the grand jury. That's all it took for him to turn his back on two thousand years of silence by his church. He gave America, did this Father Hands, the first look at how the Catholic church until now has been able to sneak and slide through trouble.

He gave his Long Island diocese profound chest pains. The next day, Caldwell called Hands and thanked him profusely for his honesty. Say anything to soothe a guy who could start remembering more and wipe everybody out. Caldwell said that he knew Hands's pain. He told him to continue to work with the therapists. Anybody but a detective or lawyer. Caldwell said that he had told all of this to Placa and Alesandro, who was the acting administrator of the diocese, but did nothing in response.

Bishop Murphy was already appointed and was busy planning his welcoming party. His aides didn't want to tell anybody else, anyone, anything until after the party.

Hands said, "Frank Caldwell said that during the first week after the party he told Bishop Murphy that, you know, Monsignor Ribaudo, a very prominent priest in the diocese, well, when he worked in high school, Father Hands said that he had repeatedly touched him in a sexually explicit way in his office and what do we do about it?"

"I was told by Monsignor Caldwell that at that point he [Ribaudo] was put on medical leave.

"I was then told by Monsignor Caldwell that in December of 2001 that Bishop Murphy wanted to ask me to seek laitization . . . to leave the priesthood, that was in everybody's best interests. I told him that I already had made that determination. Then he told me, do you know that Monsignor Ribaudo was really evaluated and we want to reinstate him back in the parish to be the monsignor in charge of St. Dominic's parish and high school before Christmas.

"And I then was told that the only way that this could happen is if I promised never to talk about it, to never tell anyone."

Caldwell asked Hands who he had told his secrets to besides his therapist. The answer was in the manner of a mortar attack.

A. (by Hands) I said well, the residential treatment community of everybody at St. Luke's. I would have to be in large group meetings and tell everybody everything that happened in my life, that that's an important part of therapy is making that kind of disclosure and dealing with the emotions around the disclosure, and I would continue to do that.

They said, well, in your legal dealings would you not tell anyone? I said well, I don't see a reason why I'm going to have to tell anybody, tell the judge. But in my case, if I'm ever asked I'm certainly not going to lie.

I think, in telling my story to a judge, I would want to say as some sense of understanding of sexual boundaries that were broken between myself and the boy, that growing up as a teenager is a very intensely vulnerable emotional place, having had sexual boundaries violated by a priest, I did impact judgments and decisions that happened with the boy that I see as very distorted and wrong and hurtful now. But to understand what happened I would someday probably want to mention that I had this experience.

Caldwell tried. "Could you say that I was a significant adult in the boy's life and not mention that I was a priest?" Hands said, "I said I would try that. I don't believe that a judge or district attorney would let it rest with that. They would want to know who actually was this person I was with." Caldwell said, "I see, I see."

Hands was preoccupied with the word *incarceration* and life thereafter. He told Caldwell to tell the bishop that he was not going to fight being ousted as a priest with him and the Vatican. The bishop was concerned about this. He wanted to know what Hands would do.

Hands knew exactly what he wanted to do. "I wonder, you know, would the bishop and the diocese help me to make that transition, meaning financially. I own nothing. I have nothing. I've been here, I have no place to stay, and medical insurance would drop me." When he mentioned this to Caldwell, he was assured that heaven, hell, and the diocese would be moved to pay his medical insurance, get him therapeutic help and pay for his transition from priesthood to regular life.

Hands said, "I then was told that it was very important that I also give them my silence around Bud Ribaudo." They were trying to get assurances that Hands would commit what amounts to perjury if asked. Not once did the diocese stop, think, and then issue a novel defense: the truth. From the Vatican through Boston and Louisville and all of New York and in all the places where the church was confronted with pedophiles, they had one answer. Lie. If it is noon in New York, it is six at night in the Vatican. The evening lie there becomes a noon lie in New York. The church is truly universal.

In the deposition, Hands recalled, "I finally told my mother and father what happened and they were understandably upset and my mother had mentioned to a friend visiting them in Florida, something about this, and word from that conversation got back to someone, who told Monsignor Caldwell. And he wanted me to call my mother or he would call my mother himself and stress with her the importance of keeping this silent because Bud Ribaudo was now back in St. Dominic's parish and they wanted to keep him back in the parish."

The bishop reinstated Ribaudo, who at first denied the allegations of molestation but later acknowledged before a grand jury that he had abused at least twelve boys.

Once you get into lying and cheating, there is no end.

A guy who worked in the diocesan office told me what put the place into cold fear. "If we don't put Ribaudo back, I don't know. You hate to think he would act against us. He does have this personal group that contributes so much, millions really, on his say-so. What if he tells his people not to contribute because we are harming him for no reason? We can't show them his mental evaluation. That's medical records. He can stay out there and claim the charge against him is a lie, that we want his job for somebody we know. He would hold that against the bishop. Maybe he could stop people from giving money to us."

So they put him back in December.

Then on a Sunday morn some weeks later, when the newspaper arrived with the story of Hands's sworn statement, Ribaudo had to leave for the second time. It was February, and he was out forever.

At the end of his last mass, the crowd stood and applauded. The people who loved him cried all the way home from mass. They shrieked over the phone to newspaper writers involved in the story. One taped message said: "You are maligning one of Christ's very best. You should burn forever for this."

Many were in tears. One who failed to cry was Stephanie Van Wie, mother of two in St. Dominic's grammar school. Standing now in a pew of tears, she smelled smoke. There is a fire here someplace, she told herself. Suddenly, people with kids were talking about Ribaudo. "One?" a friend of hers said. "I know of five boys myself."

She was born and raised in Howard Beach and Ozone Park, in Queens, and was baptized on famous 101st Avenue. The church was St. Mary Gate of Heaven. On that street the standard for acceptance of weeping as an excuse was set one day by Mr. Sal Reale. A gambling debtor tried tears in place of payment. He said he couldn't pay because he was getting married. Sal told him, "I hope you plan to walk down the aisle and not go down in a wheelchair."

Stephanie began asking and counting. She was up to ten boys and heard there were two more boys who had been molested by Ribaudo. His medical report now was getting around.

The replacement, Monsignor John Alesandro, arrived. He had been part of the three-man intervention team that first replaced and then put Ribaudo back, claiming he had been cured. The intervention team consisted of Alesandro, Monsignor Frank Caldwell, and Monsignor Alan Placa, who had to leave when he was hit with charges of molestation. The newspaper now said that they routinely paid off victims and seemed to use a railroad timetable to move priests about.

On February 9, 2003, the new pastor, Alesandro, came out fighting against all the stories about molesting. He said that the former pastor, Ribaudo, was innocent beyond saintliness, that the newspaper practices yellow journalism, and the newspaper columnist, Breslin, was a liar, a Catholic basher. No, a Catholic hater. Alesandro walked outside to shake hands.

At that hour, in the newspaper office, people were carefully going through a 181-page report of the Suffolk County Grand Jury that had just been received. Its conclusion read, "The spotlight shining on the diocese from the outside world is the only thing that caused them to change their behavior.

"The Grand Jury states, priests assigned to and working for the Diocese of Rockville Centre committed criminal acts including Rape, Sodomy, Sexual Abuse, Endangering the Welfare of Children, Use of a Child in Sexual Performance. Not one priest in the diocese who knew about these criminal acts reported them to any law enforcement agency."

The grand jury report appeared in *Newsday* on Monday morning, February 10, only hours after Alesandro's attack on the paper. He immediately went to Puerto Rico. The next Sunday, one priest, the Reverend Malcolm Burns, young and tall, out of a seminary in Houston, Texas, which seemed to have poured more spirit into him than anything he could get from his own diocese, told the parishioners at mass, "I am not even sure I believe in my own life as a priest right now." He then read the Gospel, which was about a leper begging Jesus to cure him.

Burns said, "I want to pray with you on my knees." He walked from the lectern to the lower altar step. He got down on his knees in front of the crowd and said, "A leprosy is among us and priests need to be cleansed."

He is tall and powerful-looking, with a striking Irish face, as open as a pleasant field, and short dark hair. Afterwards, he said that his mother had said to him, "Why are you suffering with this? Come back home, your room is made up. You can stop the pain and marry somebody nice."

"I would leave my husband for him," a woman with Stephanie said.

"Stop that."

"Today," she said.

A week later, outside the church, greeting parishioners, was Monsignor John Alesandro, the new pastor. Absolutely marvelous.

He was back from a vacation in Puerto Rico and wanted everybody to see his great tan. In time of crisis, calm yourself by living rich.

By April of 2004, they were scheduling a mass meeting to get rid of him.

The view of a church in trouble was different in criminal court in Brooklyn, in whose crowded hallways a space of two feet is as luxurious as the five-acre zoning of Oyster Bay. In one day, there were two priests in different courtrooms. I thought that I could make both places and watch, a tomcat near a birdbath. One of the priests, a Nigerian, Udegbulem, was due in the courtroom of Judge Firetog on the fifth floor. The other, Nelson, from India, was to be in Judge Tomei's on the third floor. I started by going to the third floor. There was no Judge Tomei. I went back down to the lobby to ask. Nobody knew. A court officer said I had to go to the tenth floor and ask the Criminal Court clerk. The elevator is so crowded that the only way to get on is to push with both hands, elbows straight, and act like you didn't do it. And you were not pushing around opera patrons. The elevator stops at every floor. The ride to the tenth is stifling and hard on the back.

I was told that Judge Tomei was on the ninth floor. Now I had to think. Nelson was in for a hearing on evidence. That would take time. Udegbulem was scheduled only for an appearance on the fifth floor. I better see him first and after that, catch some of Nelson's hearing.

I took the elevator down to the fifth floor. Slow as you can go.

In the hall outside the courtroom, a lawyer is talking to a woman.

"How can my husband have seven charges?" she says.

"Well," the lawyer starts.

"He only robbed the store once," she says.

"Yes, but when he robbed the furniture store, he also robbed six customers who were there. So they say each person he robbed is a crime."

"That's not fair," she says. "He just robbed the furniture store once."

I'm supposed to be here over religion.

The courtroom is as crowded as a subway. There are people under arrest taking up the spectators' seats. I wind up on a seat in front. I don't know if it's a regular bench or a packing case. I am in so tight, and now right in front of me a lawyer is up and he is saying to the judge:

"I am told that my client wants to relieve me as his attorney. I advised my client that I felt the case would be very difficult to win. I don't think we can win it. I advised him to accept the district attorney's plea offer."

A short man jumps up.

"I don't want him for my lawyer. He says I'm going to lose. I want a lawyer who says I'm going to win."

There is a thin man sitting alone in the last row. He wears a gray suit that looks like religious streetwear. I go back and ask him if he is Cyriacus Udegbulem. He is of color, here from Nigeria and charged with raping a woman at Our Lady of Charity church on Dean Street, which he denies.

"You are a journalist, you can find out who I am," he says.

It was strange seeing him here. Always, law enforcement in Brooklyn was founded on the principle that priests in Brooklyn never were given traffic tickets. But a strong complaint came in about Cyriacus Udegbulem. He left town and made it to Laredo, Texas. The district attorney had a couple of detectives watching him there until the grand jury in Brooklyn returned an indictment. At the same time, I was in Dallas, where the American bishops droned on, doing nothing, which is the church's way of surviving for two thousand years. I intended to fly from Dallas to Laredo and write about the arrest. I didn't. He was arrested later.

At the time of writing, Udegbulem is awaiting a second trial after a Brooklyn Supreme Court jury reached a deadlock and was unable to agree on whether he had consensual sex with the parishioner or raped her.

Up on the ninth floor, the place was empty except for a court officer who told me that Nelson had been there for a short appearance and they would be back on Thursday. When I show up again, Nelson was there and so was the judge.

In May of 1999, Father Francis X. Nelson, a thirty-nine-year-old visiting priest from India, who had been assigned to St. Mary Star of the Sea in the Cobble Hill section of Brooklyn, paid a visit to a sick woman in his parish. He then went into an empty room and pulled the woman's twelve-year-old granddaughter onto his lap. He put a hand on her breast and let his genitals touch her.

When he left, the girl told her grandmother, who informed the rest of the family. They took the complaint to the diocese of Brooklyn. They were assured that the priest was being sent off and that the bishop himself would pray for them.

The priest fled.

In Brooklyn, Bishop Thomas Daily took over a fifty-year policy of hiding any priest in trouble on a sexual act and secretly placing him in another parish. Daily had an assistant, Monsignor Otto Garcia, who was the rug man: putting so many cases under the rug that walking in the diocese offices was risky for the ankles. The young victims who were abused into lifelong damage counted for nothing.

Daily told the district attorney, "I am not a policeman. I am a shepherd."

Assistant District Attorney Dino Amoroso asked the diocese where the priest Nelson could be found. The church lawyer, Kevin Kearney, said he did not know where Father Nelson was. They believed him to be in India.

"We'd like to call the bishop in India," Amoroso said.

"We'll have to pass it through Bishop Daily," Kearney said.

Amoroso's notes remember them saying that it was doubtful if they could get Bishop Daily before day's end, but they certainly could talk to him in the morning. Dino remembers that the morning call never came. Then lawyer Kearney called from his car and shouted angrily, "We're trying to get the information. You have to wait until we get to them. The last we heard he was in India."

Meanwhile, in Nelson's former parish on Court Street, Star of the Sea, letters to Nelson were left at the church and sent to Nelson at a parish in Harlem, where he had been for a couple of years. This got to a detective, who told Amoroso, "That guy is in Manhattan. At St. Charles Borromeo. On 142nd Street."

Amorso called the New York archdiocese office on First Avenue and the auxiliary bishop said, no, they never heard of this priest Nelson. But after a couple of more calls, James McCabe, the lawyer for the archbishop, said the priest was in Harlem, but that there had never been any notice from Brooklyn about sexual allegations when Nelson moved to Manhattan.

In Brooklyn, they used Frank DeRosa, the press secretary, to announce, "the New York archdiocese was aware that there was an allegation of sexual abuse."

Suddenly, at ten o'clock at night, a fax from Bishop Daily's office was received at the archdiocese headquarters on First Avenue in Manhattan. It was dated with the year 2000, and it said that there had been charges made in the Brooklyn parish of St. Mary Star of the Sea against Father Nelson.

Nelson was told to leave the rectory in Harlem and walk down the street at 6:30 A.M. and detectives from Brooklyn would be there to meet him. Now he sat in this courtroom in the State Supreme Court in Brooklyn, charged with two counts of sexual abuse, misdemeanors, and one of endangering the welfare of a child. Obstruction of justice by the diocese officials, a serious charge, was not considered. He was subsequently convicted of the two misdemeanor counts of sexual abuse.

When Udegbulem's rape trial was on, a juror suddenly told the judge that his mother had been raped. The jury deadlocked over whether Udegbulem had forced the woman and this caused a mistrial. They would have to try him again and, after a retrial, he was acquitted.

I can state authoritatively that most real church Catholics thought of these cases as isolated crimes caused by religious *shippers*—priests of color in from another world to fill in temporarily. Hardly. The wondrous plan in Rome is to fill the empty parishes all over the world,

America first, with South Americans and Africans so black and so aggressive that the worshippers will tramp into the churches like infantry.

There are few blacks in the church pews right now, but soon the church hopes you will have a black face looking down from almost every pulpit. The Vatican people, who read only of the long past, obviously feel that the influence of St. Augustine of Hippo still can be found in people in Africa. In the South Jamaica neighborhood of Queens County, the church of St. Monica was the first color test for the parishioners, perhaps in the city. The worshippers were Italian. There was a fresh young priest one Sunday and he began by telling people about their St. Monica. She was the mother of St. Augustine, he said. "Saint Augustine was African. But I don't think we know that his mother, St. Monica, was African."

Through the rows came the muttering, "Africano!" The next week, most of the Italians had gone over to nearby St. Pius.

If the masses think that they are getting their vision of a Harlem black, a Catholic Reverend Al Sharpton, laughing and singing, they know even less about people of color than they show in their daily lives.

Up to the podium at the commencement of Georgetown University's class of 2003 came Francis Cardinal Arinze, once of Nigeria, now a Vatican yes-pope. He is not up there for a long breath when the word was all over the audience that the cardinal was a contender for becoming the next pope, the first black pope and the first pope from Africa. Both wrong. He hasn't been in Africa in twenty years. The cardinal, however, has been part of the scheming in the back rooms of the Vatican.

And now the cardinal started, "Nearly a thousand young people are graduating. To you, dear young friends, I say: Allow serious religion to lead you to lasting joy.

"In many parts of the world the family is under siege. It is opposed by an antilife mentality as is seen in contraception, abortion, infanticide, and euthanasia. It is scorned and banalized by pornography, desecrated by fornication and adultery, mocked by homosexuality, sabotaged by irregular unions, and cut into two by divorce."

He was up there trying to get his head under a papal hat by proving that a black out of Africa can make the pope's conservative Eastern Europe brand of religion remain alive. He scolded American looseness. Nowhere did the cardinal say that in his former country, Nigeria, the priests rape nuns as if they're supposed to.

By now, students were walking out on him. A couple of days later, Dean Jane Dammen McAuliffe of Georgetown wrote a letter to the class of 2003. She said many found Arinze's remarks to be exclusionary and hurtful. "I am proud to serve at a Catholic Jesuit university that prizes respect, inclusion, and academic freedom as central to our identity," she wrote, and continued in the same way.

Chapter Eighteen

My faith, my belief, the beginnings of a faith strong enough to let me ignore any debt I have to this Catholic church, originally comes out of following my aunt through St. Benedict Joseph Labre church at 94-24 118th Street in Richmond Hill, in Queens. I took a walk back on that street to see if I still experienced anything, if I could walk off and stay off. There are two red brick buildings, a rectory and convent, on either side of a brick church. In the rear is a grammar school. Sitting on the stoop of the convent were two young women of color. In all the years of decent Catholicism in Richmond Hill, there never even was a cleaning woman of that color. The street was off Atlantic Avenue, which was dreary, but the church was surrounded by large old Richmond Hill houses that quickly ran into small tight-attached two-story frame houses.

On the doorway, under a plaque saying simply CONVENT, was a sign, HOUR PLACE, that stands for the hour that women in prisons are given with their babies. Here, it stood for a halfway house for women just out of prison or on work release. Once, this was the convent for eighteen Sisters of St. Joseph, who taught in the grammar school.

A light-haired young woman named Elana was in the soundless hallway. In the first room on the left were four cribs. It was Sunday, and the mothers had the children out for a few hours with families.

On the right was a room with three computers. Elana said she was just leaving to take the subway over to the Hour Children main office in Long Island City. She was having trouble with her work release. She is out of the state Bayview women's facility in Manhattan, a hideous-looking building on the empty sidewalks of 12th Avenue. Upstairs, the nun in charge, Sister Carole Lessard, sat in a room at the head of the stairs. I guessed she was in her forties. She wore a housedress and sat with a blackened knee from surgery and an aluminum cane. She mentioned that my old grammar school had three hundred pupils, half the number when I was there. One hundred fifty are Sikh, she said.

"That nice young woman downstairs has some trouble," I said.

"Elana cleans at Kennedy Airport for thirty dollars a day," the nun said. "She worked four days. So she was getting one hundred and twenty dollars a week. Work release allows her to earn only one hundred and ten dollars a week. When the supervisors at Bayview looked at her pay stub and they saw one hundred twenty, they took ten dollars off her state benefits. They became generally restless about her.

"They do nothing to assist these women," she was saying. "They treat one small matter like this as if she had committed a new crime. No wonder the girls relapse."

The head of Hour Children, Sister Tesa Fitzgerald, was out. She runs a couple of these houses out of an office at St. Rita's church in Long Island City. The first time I met her I was tempted to taunt her, as she was the same order that taught me in grammar school. They had ruled, never start a sentence with and, so, but, and because. All I then need trying to write is handcuffs.

I never said it that day because she introduced me to Melita Oliveira. Melita told me that in 1987, she came back to Kennedy

Airport from a trip home to Peru and the customs people found five and a half ounces of cocaine in her luggage. Kids come back from holidays to Princeton with double that. Under the Rockefeller Law in New York, there is a mandatory jail term of fifteen years. She had five children in a house in Paterson, over in New Jersey. Say goodbye to them all, the judge said.

It took so long before Sister Fitzgerald of St. Benedict Joseph Labre church, touring the women's prison at Bedford Hills, noticed the state number, indicating the length of sentence, on Melita's blouse. "That number is too old," the nun said. She began a campaign to get Melita released. At the end, she went to the Cardinal of New York, John O'Connor. He was the greatest pro-labor cleric ever to hold his job. Nobody brushed off his signature on a request.

One day in Bedford Hills, two women from the administration office came to Melita's cell and told her to sit down.

"You believe in God?" one of them said.

"Yes," Melita said.

"Do you pray?"

"Yes."

"Do you ask God for something?"

"Yes."

"Do you pray to get out of prison?"

"Yes."

"God is good. He gave you clemency. A pardon. We just heard."

"Scream," one of the administrators said.

"I can't," Melita said.

"I'll scream for you," the woman said. She opened the door and let a shriek go down the prison hall. Soon the hall was packed. Melita had a pardon, everybody shouted.

Melita was still in the Long Island City headquarters on this day. And I thought that if I stayed here in the convent long enough somehow I would wind up scrubbing floors and other chores. Getting anybody out of prison gives you the credentials to make demands of the nearest bystander.

Outside, the sidewalk was empty for it was between the end of the eleven-thirty mass and the one-thirty, which was in Spanish.

And it is here, today, in the church and school of my origins, where the lives of nuns in the convent are now dedicated to getting women out of prison and helping them afterwards, here suddenly on this empty sidewalk I was never prouder of anything in my life. This is where I come from.

I then went into the church. It was dim and so much smaller than I remembered it. And after the nuns next door, who follow the life of Christ, the church and its saints I never knew seemed desolate. I had been told that the pastor is a fine man, far from the past. But it might be late for me. By tradition, as you get older you draw closer to the church. It looks like I am going another way.

Immediately, just by walking half a block, the world tells you that this club of old men, this Catholic church that refuses to open its arms for so much good, makes it preposterous, and in my book flat evil. Only down the street from St. Benedict's is the old yellow Methodist church, which now is the Sikh headquarters for all of New York. Much of their church was burned down. The Sikhs rebuilt. The street on this day was lined with their jobs, yellow cabs, and the sidewalk was crowded with men wearing turbans who stood with bare feet glistening wet from stepping into one of a line of water buckets. Children padded about in wet bare feet. Many shoes of all kinds were in neat lines on tables along the front of the church buildings. It looked like a tag sale, but the bare feet said they belonged to worshippers. Turbans, bare feet, women in saris that took in the entire color wheel, strange language being spoken. I thought they needed a white steer with people walking around him in respect.

A man named Prem Pal Singh, one of the Sikh leaders, introduced himself. He said he teaches at Franklin K. Lane High School. He is from Punjab, a province in a corner of India, which is where the Sikh faith was founded. He explained that the faithful worship in bare feet in honor of the holy book, which was written in the sixteenth century in Punjab. It is 1,478 pages.

"Eighty percent of the Sikhs drive taxis and the others own gas stations," he said. This wasn't a statistic thrown into a conversation. Much of the Sikh belief was based on working, he said.

As it should be with the church up the street.

St. Francis of Assisi: *Laborare est orare.* Work is prayer.

He went to a table and returned with a booklet. I thanked him, and as I walked down the street, I read some of it:

Philosophy and Beliefs: There is only one God. He is the same God for all people of all religions. . . . The true path to achieving salvation and merging with God does not require renunciation of the world by celibacy, but living the life of a householder, earning an honest living and avoiding wordly temptations and sins.

Sikhism condemns blind rituals such as fasting, visiting places of pilgrimage, superstitions, worship of the dead, idol worship, etc.

Sikhism preaches that people of different races, religions or sex all are equal in the eyes of God. It teaches the full equality of men and women. Women can participate in any religious function.

Sikhs do not have priests . . . they had become corrupt and full of ego. Sikhs only have custodians and any Sikh is free to read the holy book. . . .

Here is a faith from Punjab in a corner of India that believes that God made all equal, man and woman, that celibacy is bad and women, who are created the same as men, are therefore equal in every respect, including in the religion.

I'm from the church that has had two thousand years to think and consider and is in the great cities of the world and the church segregates, despises, and fears women.

As I write, I have beside me stacks of books about Catholicism that become higher each time I go out for a walk and pass a bookstore. My problem with the books is that they go deeply into the traceable church, the lives of the popes and those of the best saints, always done with the most pompous, boring language. The one book I could not wait to read was about Mary Magdalene, whom I believe to be the best of anything Christ had around him. She went to the last mile while all these men ran like dogs. They call her a prostitute, a whore. Some whore, the last person walking with Christ, with any luck, you'll know you're near heaven when you get a glimpse of her telling people what to do, a whore owns half of heaven.

So I buy the book on Mary Magdalene and get no description of her real life and I put it down.

A friend asks me from nowhere, "Do you remember 'churching'?"

He didn't have to say anything else. Churching was a practice of the religion in which a mother after birth couldn't enter a church until purified by some special prayers during a service.

I cringed. I shook my head like a dog throwing off water. It was impossible that I ever let my late wife be humiliated like this, be openly humiliated. I tried to remember the baptisms of my six children. I ran through as many scenes as I could. Who was at the house? Who went to church with the baby? Who was the godfather and the godmother? All right. I can see them. Now, was the mother in church? I tried to see her. Or explain the absence by saying that Italian women always did stay home and cook during the baptism. I don't know. Five baptisms. The first was for twins, James and Kevin. The more I looked the more I saw her only at home taking a baby from somebody who came in from church with him. Did she ever go to this churching ceremony? That better not have happened.

I asked John Powis, "Do they still have churching?"

"Lord, no," he said.

"He told me that he was going to marry me in heaven," Barbara Blaine called out.

She was complaining that when priests love women rather than young boys, their immaturity fits a high school lunchroom rather than anyplace that adults go.

She said that her priest said they could run around down here on earth and he would make an honest woman out of her up in the skies.

Barbara Blaine was across the street from a big bishop's conclave in Dallas, running her meeting of victims of priests, and women who insist on being ordained as priests. It was one of the many bishops' meetings in which they got nothing done except room service.

The meetings of bishops were supposed to settle forever the molesting of the young by priests and harboring of child molesters probably on up to the same bishops sitting there. Estimates around the nation ran as high as twenty-five thousand cases of young men being molested. And that is the number, the great minority, who got themselves to the point of admitting what happened to them. Nothing was done. Watching the bishops file into the meeting room, the idea burned into you: Put out a scale and have the bishops weigh in and declare the avoirdupois champion of the second meeting of Catholic molesters. The results might give an indication of whether weight has anything to do with the crumbling of will against temptation.

That is not as silly as the bishops holding two meetings about the crisis of their church and not once facing the truth, that if they remain all male there will be a choirboy and his father in the police station signing a complaint against a parish priest as long as we all live.

My friend Fran Kissling, running her meeting that made the bishops across the street uncomfortable, has gone through years of old fearful churchmen in their black suits lying to her, shunning her. Fran Kissling was a nun in New York who left to run Catholics for Free Choice. In 1984 she had four priests and twenty-eight nuns sign a full-page ad in the *New York Times* newspaper calling for free choice in abortions. The Vatican erupted and demanded retractions or dismissals.

"Four of the signers quit us right away," Fran was saying.

"The four men."

There was also Louise Haggett, whose CITI Ministries—Celibacy Is The Issue—called for the end of celibacy and gender requirements for becoming a priest. The thing about these outside groups of Catholic women and girls is that at first they might seem small and peripheral. But the energy and arithmetic says they must win. Only the oldest, most ignorant Catholic could say these women won't drive everybody out who gets in their way. The CITI group shows married Protestant ministers have been ordained as Catholic priests since 1980, and their families were moved into rectories from which priests who married were evicted. She also showed that there was a couple of thousand priests involved in sexual abuse. While that may sound horrible, it is an abysmally low number. The guilty who escape are at least as numerous. Half the Catholics in the world have no regular priests and fifty-three hundred parishes in the United States are without a priest. Ms. Haggett said that there are twenty-five thousand priests who have left the church in order to marry. Her pamphlets called for them to be brought back immediately, and the celibacy and gender rules for new priests thrown out.

Also spread on a table at both meetings were the pamphlets from the Women-Church Convergence of Chicago. It said, "Women's voices have been conspicuously absent among victim survivors even though experts on clergy abuse believe troubled priests and other clergy are more likely to abuse females, especially adult women. In a system that keeps secrets and dishonors women, it is no small wonder that the claims taken seriously come from boys and men, despite well-documented cases of women of all ages, including nuns, subject to sexual abuse and even rape by churchmen."

All these years later and Fran Kissling, her hair white now, passes out enough reports to either reform the church or put everybody in jail. Right across the street in their meeting were these bishops, all of them looking like roast beef dinner, who sat and said nothing and did nothing and never would. And their precious canon law, as was spelled out in court in Dublin, Ireland, was as meaningful as the rules of the Winged Foot Country Club or wherever else they get a rich guy to take them out for a round.

Instead of looking at themselves, these bishops and cardinals whirl about and point and snarl, "Gays. Homosexuals." One of the bosses at St. Patrick's Cathedral, Clark, got up at ten o'clock mass one Sunday and roared against homosexuals. Get rid of them and that would be the cure for everything.

I had coffee one evening with Ted Welsh, who spent many years in the Jesuits and was talking about how from nowhere all the years came back to him the other day.

"I don't know why it came up, but somebody handed me a phone number for a man I was in the Jesuits with and I had not heard from him in many years, so I don't know why they gave me his number but I took it. So here I was with a slip of paper that represented three decades of my life. I had not seen the man or talked to him in seventeen years. His middle name is Edward and we will leave it at that. Yes, of course I once had feelings for him and I'm pretty sure he had feelings for me.

"But we never even touched hands.

"I was eighteen when I went into the seminary at Dallas. I took a vow of poverty, chastity, and obedience. Celibacy at eighteen is, I believe, nuts. I was transferred to Spring Hill College in Alabama, I copied books for art at Spring Hill. They questioned me on that. 'What kind of an adviser would you be to people?'

"We were never alone. Somebody always watched us. Masturbation was the worst transgression you could perpetrate. I knew I had feelings for men, but you couldn't touch anybody. You don't really want to explore. You're a restricted person. You're always watched. There would be people eating on their knees as a punishment, but you never knew if it was for sex.

"What changed everything for me was reading about the Stonewall Riot. I was at the Boston Theological Institute and we saw the *Village Voice*. That was in June of 1969, right? The police went in for a homo raid. Because many of us had been in South America we knew the one story of the man being arrested for being gay. They found he had no immigration papers and they were turning him over to the immigration people. He jumped out of the police station third floor and was impaled on the spiked iron fence. There was cause to riot. All these gays chased the cops out of the bar and started rioting in the streets. It went on for three nights, I believe. I know all these closets came open, except of course mine.

"I was sent to the Apostolic school at Loyola in Los Angeles. The rector carried an umbrella on sunny days. If women came near him, he opened the umbrella in their faces and crossed the street.

"I then went to Loyola of New Orleans again. I saw my friend, Edward. He saw me, I think he knew I was gay. I didn't know if he was. We never touched. We talked. He wanted to teach theology. I wanted to work in South America. We had a class on Kierkegaard and the professor became so overwhelmed by Kierkegaard that he burst into tears. So did we. There were some times when I could not bear to be near him during a day. I stayed completely clear of him. At the end of the semester, we were at a large camp, closely supervised. We went out in shallow bottom boats and caught water moccasins. They were long, mud-colored, and had cottonmouths. We put them in a barrel when we caught them. We used a long pole with an aluminum claw to put them into a sack. Two of us held open the sack and the third fellow was pushing the snakes in. We had thirty snakes. On the way back the fangs were pushing through the sacks and hanging out. The two of us were exhilarated. An older faculty man, who knew, came out with a club and killed them. He said one bite and we could be through.

"At the end of the week, the two of us looked at each other. He was going to Chicago. I was going to Mexico. We did not even shake hands. He said good-bye. I said good-bye. We both left. I had a hollow feeling. I knew I could never last as a priest. I left the order in 1985 and began working in school programs.

"I was in New York at a gay club one night. I was leaning against the wall watching the dance. Being fourteen again. This man next to me said, 'Do you want to dance?' I said yes. His name was Manny. He was in his Wall Street clothes. We danced and talked. He said he had to leave. I stayed on. I turned around, and he was back. He asked me, 'Do you want to have dinner?' I said yes. We went to the Sevilla, near Christopher and Bleecker, and had sangria and paella. He said to me, 'I'm not interested in a short-term romance.' I said, 'Neither am I.' There you are. I told my father about it, and he said, 'Anybody you love is good for us. Bring him home.' Seventeen years Manny and I have been together. And now I'm handed this note. I asked, 'What is this area code?' They said, 'Nashville. He is at Vanderbilt

University. Teaching history.' I don't know how I felt. I just called. He said he had been married three times. 'Are you with anyone?' I said, 'Yes, a man. For seventeen years.' He said, 'That's great. That's the way it should be.' I agreed. Then he said, 'What were those days about?'

"We left each other on that question. We had no answer."

Chapter Nineteen

The first fires of protest, actually flames for decorative candles, started with a meeting of about one hundred fifty priests to form a group called Voice of the Ordained. It was similar to the parishioners' Voice of the Faithful, which held a large meeting in Boston.

Each was like an early primary. Everything seemed far off and yet it was so close. The priests met at Queens College, because they were not allowed on church property by order of the bishop, Thomas Daily, who regarded a meeting as a threat to the existence of the church and, besides, you have one formal meeting and the next one is in a grand jury and after that you wind up in a courtroom, and this was something to be avoided, things being what they are, specifically with Daily, who comes out of Boston, where he protected his young by writing a congratulatory note to Father John Geoghan, one of the worst of all pedophiles.

Powis started the meeting in Queens by saying, "I received a call from a reporter who wasn't familiar with us, and he said to me, 'Are you a mon-seen-yore? Is that between a priest and a bishop?' "

Powis said, "I told him, 'It's one of the things that must go.' "

Powis said, "We have to get away from the hierarchy and go back to Vatican II. Why do we have women sitting and counseling and then let priests take over and say the mass and hear confessions?"

At a glance the meeting seemed innocuous, older men in day-time civilian clothes at a meeting. But this was the first expression of decency demanding its way that has been seen in the church in America in our time.

Here were these men who had spent their lives as priests and now had been betrayed. Powis sat in his St. Barbara's and had four-teen appointments a day with people whose children stray, whose rent is unpaid, whose job has been lost. One woman said her son had told the police about drug peddlers in the building and the police thanked him profusely and then blurted out the kid's name to the drug dealers and now she feared for the son's life, and rightly so. There was Bryan Karvelis, who had a severe kidney operation but still conducted his church, the Transfiguration, in Williamsburg, Brooklyn. He announced, "My shillelagh makes a lot of noise and touches the hearts of those who left. It can bring about a rebirth of our church."

He also meant recalling priests who had left to be married. One in the room who was on the committee was Thomas McCabe. His ministry was at the Farragut Houses in Flatbush. A nun, Sister Eileen, was stationed there. They commited the unpardonable sin of falling in love and marrying. They left the religious life. To lose McCabe, everybody at the meeting said, was disheartening. "Why can't he just come back?" somebody asked. See your church, Powis said.

The speaker was Eugene Kennedy, a Jesuit out of Loyola University of Chicago, who since has left the priesthood, has married, and writes quite successfully. His *The Unhealed Wound,* about sexuality in the church, is the best work on homosexuals in the church.

Years before, I had introduced him to Jacqueline Kennedy, when she was at the Viking Press, where I was published, and it led to Eugene Kennedy's first major book, on Mayor Richard Daley of Chicago. A couple of times he came to my house in Forest Hills and said mass at the kitchen table for my wife when she was ill.

He told the crowd that he had suggested a meeting of all the hierarchy with Father Theodore Hesburgh, the former president of Notre Dame and whose reputation goes beyond religion and race. He is the dominant Catholic figure in America. "He would give credibility that they couldn't," Kennedy said. "Of course they wouldn't want to be in the same room with Ted Hesburgh. The truth would drive them out the door."

Kennedy said, "We stepped on a land mine. And our leaders gave up scapegoats. We have learned one thing out of this, that you cannot divide people into higher and lower parts. There is an evil to force such distinctions on people. The church hierarchy is forcing its will on all below them. And when this pressing reaches the bottom, it could produce a stumbling priest intimidating the young and vulnerable and causing the vilest of crimes."

"You don't have to pull the walls down. They are falling by themselves," Kennedy said.

Afterwards, we went to the Sly Fox on Union Turnpike and had a glass of wine. I happened to bring up the subject of women and he looked at me in surprise. How could you ask about such a thing? "There will be no church without women," he said.

The Voice parishioners in Boston's first big meeting was in a hotel auditorium because their Cardinal Law refused to let them anywhere near a church.

The meeting in Boston drew forty-two hundred Catholics in the Hynes Auditorium, the one largest gathering of Catholics protesting in five hundred years. A sign in the crowd outside said that Cardinal Law should resign by September 22. "My birthday," Rick Webb, holding the sign said. It didn't happen quite that fast. A couple of paces away, Stephen Lewis, who said that he had been abused when he was an altar boy by a priest named Kelley, said he had been paid $10,000 and signed an agreement to keep the matter secret. "I am the first one to break the agreement," he said. He bawled into a bullhorn, "Cardinal Law is a pimp!"

This was in July 2002 and in eleven months they and *The Boston Globe* had Cardinal Law out and a new bishop, Sean Patrick O'Malley, who wore a friar's robes and would not move into Law's mansion.

The Voice meeting that started it was the work of James Muller, a physician from Wellesley who has a Nobel Prize and who out of disgust started the Voice of the Faithful five months before this with eighty people in the basement of St. John the Evangelist in Wellesley. He is a thin man, balding, and with a mild gaze. I told him that in the prizefight between Lennox Lewis and Mike Tyson, the corner man for Lewis, Emanuel Steward, told Lewis after the fourth round that Tyson was shot and that he best get rid of him right now, "before he gets the chance to get lucky." I repeated that.

"It goes beyond a prizefight," I said. "You got a cardinal here who can't stand up. Shove him and he's gone. They have a pope who thinks anything outside of Poland is a sin. But if you give them time they will get lucky. Lucky consists of waiting you out. They've gone two thousand years doing that. They will send somebody to your funeral. Don't give them the chance."

I spoke with the velocity of a truck's backfire and was sure it would excite him. Why shouldn't I be loudly passionate? I understood the grandeur of the very act of these people, standing up against the worst American clergy, their cardinal, and in turn against all of Rome with its deceit and despotism. Get rid of them before they get the chance to get lucky. Muller turned to somebody else. He said over his shoulder to me that it was fine to talk to me and we would see each other again.

A lady named Connolly from Our Lady Help of Christians in Newton said, "Isn't he a great man? A big doctor."

"What kind?"

"A cardiologist at Mass General."

"Is that what he got the Nobel for?"

"Oh, no. He got the Nobel Peace Prize. Did you ever hear of the group called Doctors to Stop Nuclear War? He was one of the leaders. He got the prize for that."

I was telling him about fighting.

The main speaker was the Reverend Thomas Doyle, who was a canon lawyer at the Vatican embassy in Washington at the first trial of pedophiles anybody heard of in this country, the trial in the Lafayette, Louisiana, diocese of the Reverend Gilbert Gauthe, who started by molesting a nine-year-old altar boy and then assaulted at least thirty-six others. The Lafayette diocese, which is outside New Orleans, paid $20 million to the families. Doyle wrote a report saying that pedophilia is "a lifetime disease with no hope at this point in time for cure."

He called out now, "What we have experienced in our lifetime is a disaster the horror of which is perhaps equaled by the bloodshed of the Inquisition but which certainly makes the indulgence scam of the Reformation pale by comparison. I submit that the sexual abuse has been a symptom of a deeper and much more destructive malady: the failure of clericalism.

"The delusion is that the clergy are above the rest, deserving unquestioned privilege and stature, the keepers of our salvation, the guarantors of our favor with the Lord. But the deadliest symptom is the unbridled addiction to power.

"No policy statements, no widespread purges will come close to repairing the immeasurable damage done to the emotions and souls of the victims and survivors and all those in the neighborhoods they come from.

"We all need to accept the responsibility for our own spiritual growth and not depend on a magical notion of sacraments and the priests and bishops who administer them."

Afterwards, people walked the six or seven blocks over to the large gray Cathedral of the Holy Cross, which now has only a few hundred people at the main Sunday masses.

There were far more gathering on the church steps in the dusk. Survivors, as they were called, stepped spontaneously into the middle of the large circle and thanked the people for their help. One woman's head bobbed into the center of the circle and her voice came clear and firm and memorable: "Until today I have been alone. I felt ashamed and guilty. The way you have treated me today has made me feel that I will never be alone again. I don't know how to thank you except to say I love you. Thank you so much."

Certainly Thomas Doyle would not last days such as this. He was thrown out of his post in Germany by an archbishop in charge of military chaplains. He was Irish, of course, Archbishop Edwin F. O'Brien. Another cheap genuflecting dullard with no understanding that he was only making Doyle's voice stronger and ready to go for more years.

He owned all the streets around him, but he could not control the calendar or his body. The Parkinson's weakened John Powis. The doctors at New York University worried about a growth on the foot. The parishioners, fifteen and sixteen a day, came into the rectory to see him about abusive husbands, an operation for a child at Woodhull Hospital, an eviction notice, a marriage, baptism, a funeral, suspended welfare payments. One earnest face after another, creased by a hard life, in trouble, trying to hope, depending on him. He was limp at the end of each day. Suddenly he was seventy years old—the retirement age in his diocese.

Much of his last weeks were consumed by Milagos Torres of 11A Menehan Street. She had eight children and an eviction notice. She had the eviction notice because she owed the rent for a couple of months or so, what do you care, she has eight children. She had a good excuse for not paying the rent. She didn't have any money. Her apartment was four leg-numbing flights up in a depressing building. At the top, here was Milagos, who smiled beautifully. She couldn't speak a word of English.

Four times, Powis went to the housing court with Milagos Torres. He had a story every time. Then the judge said to him, "I can't stall this anymore. They are going to complain about me and I'll wind up losing my job. You have to have some money the next time."

Two weeks later, Powis and Milagos showed up in court and the judge asked for money and she shook her head and Powis said, "She really doesn't have any." The judge again said he was going to lose his job if he didn't collect. Powis sighed and went into his pocket.

Now, in his sermon at his last mass at St. Barbara's, he said, "The judge had been wonderful to us. He let us go for months. But he said he had to have four thousand one hundred and sixteen dollars right here and now or he would have to order an immediate eviction. I said, 'All right.' I went into my pocket and took out a money order for a thousand dollars. Then I took out three more money orders of a thousand. Then I gave him a money order for one hundred and sixteen dollars. I said, 'Here, that is four thousand one hundred sixteen dollars.'

"And he gave me back the money, thank God."

The church roared. He didn't have to tell them that the money came right out of the collections and would have left him in deep trouble. One woman was laughing as the people around her told her what Powis was saying. She was Milagos Torres.

With two weeks to work with, Powis was able to get a foundation to get up the money and keep the woman in her house.

His sermons lately had been to instruct people on how to apply for a state program, Health Care Plus, to tell them that they must report drug locations and that they must come to the church immediately upon receipt of an eviction notice. Above all, to love the people around them. There are seventy-seven Latino soldiers from his parish in Iraq. When one of them appeared at church, Powis asked him to come up to the altar and speak to the parishioners. One of them was carried away with his patriotism and said we should fight the dirty guerrillas forever. Powis didn't care what the soldier said. He loved the young boy for being there. On another Sunday, however, one soldier got up and was speechless. He was frozen. He turned to Powis, and shaking with tears, said, "It was hell."

Now, at his last mass, the church in front of him was crowded. The adults said prayers aloud and clapped and raised their arms. In the aisles were young girls, eleven and twelve, walking primly, as if to show they were grown up. Younger children were kicking and flinging themselves around the pews. On the left side of the altar, young boys sat on the radiator cover and then threw themselves out into the air.

This was the end of John Powis's fortieth year as a priest. In his time, he has had people of every religion, and those with none, as his flock. His church in Brooklyn isn't going to get over the loss because there is nobody like him and nobody even to replace him. There are not enough priests left in Brooklyn to take over churches whose priests are over age and leaving.

"I nearly forgot," Powis called out at the end of the mass. "Are there any birthdays? Everybody with a birthday come out in the aisle and we'll sing 'Happy Birthday.' " The woman on the keyboard at the front of the church played "Happy Birthday" fast and loud and people clapped and sang lustily and wonderfully at the end of John Powis's forty-year career for his God.

On Monday morning, he walked out of the rectory with a small overnight case. He was going to a Trappist monastery outside of Worcester, Massachusetts. He had never been there, but he had heard about it and dreamed for a long time of resting in silence in a country setting.

Fran Barrett picked him up.

"Are you sure?" she said.

"Yes. I can't wait. Just get me to the bus terminal on 42nd Street."

When she got into Manhattan, she said, "I can get you to Hartford quicker than go crosstown."

She turned onto the FDR Drive and went to the New England Thruway. He protested, but not enough.

Now that she had him alone in the car, Fran Barrett said, "Do you know what you're going to do?"

"What I said. I am going to have a church without walls and a few people to help me. Then we'll have a Bushwick housing group."

"We maybe can raise money for that. But what are you going to do for money for yourself?"

"I'll be fine."

"No, you won't. How much do you have saved?"

"Nothing."

"Well, you've got to think about it and discuss it with us."

"Just let me get up there in the monastery and rest and think."

"I worry," she said.

"Don't."

"I told you what to do once and you didn't do it. It was a disaster."

Yes, it was. The Union Square Association in Manhattan gave him one of their $50,000 awards that go to activists. The rules say that $40,000 must go to the programs he worked. There was no problem getting that money spread to organizations. But the last $10,000 was a worry. "Give that away, too," Fran said.

He didn't do it right away. He held it long enough to have to pay income taxes on it. This also put him over the income limit for a studio apartment he and his sister, a nun, were renting on income subsidized terms on 14th Street in Stuyvesant Town. Powis went there for a day's sleep once a week if possible. But the $10,000 income on top of a priest's stipend put him over the income mark. The rent payment for him went up $150 a month. He didn't have it.

"What do you intend to do?" Fran asked him when they arrived in Worcester.

"Rest for three weeks," he said.

He got out of the car and walked on the road through stone pillars and up to the monastery for his rest.

That was on a Monday. That Sunday, he was back. He couldn't stand the loneliness. He also wasn't well enough to take on all the things he was talking about. He told somebody that he would be in St. Barbara's for one day a week. Then on to his other ideas. He said that they were not to tell Fran Barrett that he was back so soon.

"We're in trouble," Fran said.

He left his friend Thomas McCabe, the former priest who was in his "Voice of the Ordained." McCabe started with a thousand priests and has made it onto a national group that will multiply quickly and thus cannot be denied. Also, they are American priests, not Roman.

Then one day, as my Aunt Harriet was struggling with this sea of blurring words on a page, she suddenly snarled: "Bastard."

"Who?"

"Who? This."

The story said that a retired Catholic priest, Andrew Millar, sixty-nine, had walked into the public restroom at Tobay Beach, at the eastern end of Jones Beach, and went into a stall and sodomized a fifteen-year-old boy who had learning disabilities; the boy's father was right outside on the beach. When the boy didn't return, the father went inside and found the old priest in the stall with his son. The priest pled guilty and was awaiting sentence.

Aunt Harriet stared at the sky. "Tobay Beach. A wonderful, wonderful place. With freedom and excitement and joy. My three kids, your two boys. Now look what they've done to my wonderful, restful memories and dreams of that place."

Right away, she did one of the few positive things the Irish can do naturally: go right to the core.

"Where is he?"

"Who?"

"The pope. Where is he in this? Why doesn't he say something? Who the hell does he think he is? You don't expect me to blame some demented old priest, do you? I blame the pope."

It did not end with this one fury. Some days later, she sat in front of her flag and said her prayers and then, voice still laden with cold fury, she declared, "I'm out. Out of the former Catholic church, as I knew it."

She shuffled some papers. "The Quakers. I wrote them. They sent me this. I know they were very good in Ireland during the famine. I am thinking of transferring my faith to them."

She was still thinking about this in June when her grandson, Christopher, was arranging his marriage. There was no church involved. She gave the couple the engagement ring and wedding ring her late husband gave her fifty-eight years ago. That was the end of her years in her church. She became a lone figure on a cold, empty train platform whose sign, LAST STOP, was dimly lit, and the small bulbs on the platform lightposts placed small pools of light at a distance from each other on the cold, empty platform. She left me to the one other influence on my life and beliefs.

Epilogue

A clamor came up the staircase as I went to the basement auditorium of our Lady of Mercy church in Forest Hills. I was looking for Arlene D'Arienzo, who lives across the street from the church. She was at a table with Jason Zivkovic, who worked on a papier-mâché house. Her friend, Sister Ann Barbara Desiano, was up in front of 110 excited children in a summer Bible-study class. The nun was in the costume of a Pharaoh, a tall paper hat and a brown smock and silver paper to look like a sword hanging from a belt. The wall behind her was covered with large drawings of camels and Egyptian buildings mounted on large panels of cardboard. Arlene D'Arienzo worked on them in her house. Now, the nun was telling the story of Moses trying to get his people out of four hundred years of slavery.

"Moses said to the Pharaoh, 'Let my people go!' "

She had them all call, "Let my people go."

Then Ann Barbara Desiano read of the plagues of Egypt.

"Frogs!" the nun called out.

With this, she rushed up the aisle throwing handfuls of small rubber frogs.

And the auditorium turned into over one hundred pairs of scrambling bare legs as boys and girls went diving under the tables to collect the frogs.

She called out the next pest.

"Locusts."

The nun again pounded down the aisle, this time throwing small rubber locusts. The kids pounced on them all at once.

Then sister had them call out again, "Let my people go!"

In the laughing and excitement, Arlene D'Arienzo said quietly, "Isn't this a sweet moment?" I nodded. "This is probably too homespun for you," she said.

No. It was what the Catholics should be about. One sweet moment after the next. We know it as love. When I start my parish this is all it will be. As the children left the auditorium, I wanted to talk to Arlene about how good I am doing. Up Breslin! She was one of the reasons I began covering the sins of the church. With each story, each realization of how widespread and evil this church system was, I could boisterously proclaim my vision of becoming my own bishop with my own congregation. Good Boy Yourself, Breslin!

And now she said, "You're bad."

"What do you mean?" I asked her.

"You're very bad."

"Why?"

"You attack the church."

"You told me!"

"I never told you to do it the way you're doing it."

"What way is that?"

"Mean. You're mean. Where is your forgiveness and compassion?"

"Do they have any compassion for the people when they ruin their lives?"

"That doesn't mean you must wreck the whole church."

"What church? Do you mean a church that lets this go on?"

"Well, I'm in the church. I need the church very much for solace. I don't need you destroying it."

"You told me to."

"I told you to clean it, not wreck it."

"Then just for you, I'll stop."

"You can't."

ABOUT THE AUTHOR

JIMMY BRESLIN was awarded the Pulitzer Prize for Distinguished Commentary in 1986. Through the last four decades, his columns have appeared in various New York City newspapers and have been syndicated nationwide. He is the author of *I Want to Thank My Brain for Remembering Me* and several bestselling novels, among them *The Gang That Couldn't Shoot Straight*. He lives in New York City. Breslin currently writes a three-times-a-week column for *Newsday*.

Printed in the United States
By Bookmasters